Marty -

I thought of your time of Cancer treatments when I read pages 70-72. Your resiliency in recovery is a testament to your root system which sustains you over the long haul I think.

Anyway, glad you are bouncing back and are back at home.

Mike Wilson

1 April 2015

FLOURISHING

WHY SOME PEOPLE THRIVE WHILE OTHERS JUST SURVIVE

dr. stephen r. graves

dr. stephen r. graves
Flourishing
Published by KJK Inc. Publishing
P.O. Box 9448
Fayetteville, AR 72702

Details in some anecdotes and stories have been changed to protect the identities of the persons involved.

ISBN [[978-1-940794-03-7]]

Steve is committed to drive conversations, extract insights, and publish around four themes of personal passion and curiosity: **Leadership Development, Social Innovation, Practical Faith,** and **Organizational Strategy.** *Flourishing* is part of the Practical Faith series.

For more resources from KJK Publishing and to view Steve's blog, visit *www.stephenrgraves.com*

FLOURISHING
WHY SOME PEOPLE THRIVE WHILE
OTHERS JUST SURVIVE

EVEN THOUGH IT IS
PLANTED, WILL IT *FLOURISH*?
– EZEKIEL 17:10 (HCSB)

"How are you doing?"

We have been asked that question and have asked it in return more times than we can remember. More often than not, our response consists of some version of "I'm fine" paired with a polite smile. We don't really even think about it. It just comes out, and in that moment it's likely quite true. We may not have just won the lottery, but we aren't bleeding from a head wound either, so…we're fine.

Every once in a while, though, we get asked that same question with a slightly different tone. Maybe it's from a friend that we haven't spoken to in months, or perhaps a family member who notices that we haven't quite been ourselves lately. Suddenly, the question is loaded with new meaning. They aren't asking how we're doing at that very moment. They want to know, "How's life going?"

Often we don't even notice the change in tone and we unconsciously reply with our stock "I'm fine." Sometimes, though, our answer changes just a little bit and the slightest hesitation accompanies our words. "I'm fine…just tired." "I'm fine…just worn out." "I'm fine…I'm hanging in there."

In these little changes and in these briefest of pauses tends to be a profound truth, one that I hope to address in this book.

We are fine…and we hate being fine. We are sick of being fine. We are desperate for something more. We want to flourish.

Unfortunately, for many of us, our lives are far from flourishing. At best, we are surviving. One day to the next. One paycheck to the next. One vacation to the next.

Deep within ourselves we know that we were meant for something greater. We were meant to live meaningful, impactful lives, full of passion, joy, and sorrow. In short, we were meant to flourish.

This book is a humble attempt to help you find that life. So...I'll ask you again, "How are you doing?"

CHAPTER 1

FISTS AND
SCREAMS

*Life Is More
than Existence*

"Life is a matter of degrees. Some have life, but it flickers like a dying candle, and is indistinct as the fire in the smoking flax. Others are full of life, and are bright and vehement, like the fire upon the blacksmith's forge when the bellows are in full blast. Christ has come that His people may have life in all its fullness!" – C.H. Spurgeon

IT BEGINS AT birth. After nine months of gestation a baby is pushed into this world, fists clenched and screaming. And we've been shouting at this life ever since. Not an angry shout, but a universal groan for meaning and fulfillment; an internal cry for satisfaction and an endless search for a life worth living.

The sound may vary according to our age, personality, background, and station in life. But it's there. The intellectual woman looks down from her credentialed mountaintop and thoughtfully questions if mental firepower is really enough to bring peace and contentment in life. The adventuresome millennial pops his confused head up and wonders, *Where is this whole thing going?* The boomer competitor sits spent after another conquering achievement, but instead of being satisfied on the inside, he feels empty and unmotivated. The sentimental mom pulls herself back into the moment once more, but all the while withering on the inside and weepy for personal nourishment.

You and I both know how beautiful and ugly life can be all at once. It can be so rich and full. But it can be so exhausting and hollow as well. We get trapped into routines and the monotony of raising kids, chasing hobbies, climbing the career ladder, and as the years pass, the groan keeps rumbling in our soul. We mask it, but it's there.

In my role as a coach and adviser, I've had the occasion to ask countless business and nonprofit leaders over the past decades, "How is your life and work going?"

Too often, that's when I see "the look." It resembles a wince. It's a pained look that bespeaks disappointment and frustration. When I see "the look," I know the person I'm talking to is going to tell me about how life is not offering adequate satisfaction and fulfillment. In many cases, these are people who, on the outside, appear successful, perhaps as measured by the prestige and pay of their jobs. But deep inside, *they* know that some important areas of their lives are not measuring up to what they had hoped for or expected. Although our primary reason for engagement might be business strategy, the eventual conversation about life fulfillment comes around.

Pediatricians use the term *failure to thrive* for young children who aren't gaining weight as they should. I believe that many adults have their own kinds of failure to thrive. They're existing. They're getting by. Their lives are certainly not a complete waste. But at the same time, they aren't really thriving either. Or as I put it, they aren't *flourishing*.

+ To *not flourish* is to feel hindered, withered, exhausted, empty, hopeless, helpless, confused, purposeless, or lost.
+ To *flourish* is to bloom, grow, thrive, be energized, shine, bear fruit, break forth, or overflow.

Permit me to ask: Which description more nearly fits you?

Jesus used a phrase that I think beautifully describes the kind of life we all want: abundant life (see John 10:10). That's it! We want life that's abundant, not minimal or insignificant. We want a life of meaning, satisfaction, and sustainable richness. And here is the kicker—just because a person has met the Master and is a believer doesn't mean they are living the life God always intended for them. It's true; some just get by while others *flourish*.

That's where I will try to help.

THE ADDRESS OF THE FLOURISHING LIFE

Over my entire life, I've been captivated by the lives of people who have flourished. As a young man, I read of people like Abraham Lincoln, John Calvin, Billy Graham, and Mother Teresa, and I wondered at their fruitful lives. What made their lives so profound in impact and quality? What did they do that others did not? What did they value and what did they disdain? What formed their core and sustained their hunger?

The more I grew, the more I understood that flourishing wasn't what I once thought. It's not just being highly successful in your career. More often than not, flourishing is a whole life lived to the fullest—a focused and authentic life. Or as Fyodor Dostoevsky said it, "The mystery of human existence lies not just in staying alive but in finding something to live for."

The ability to flourish is not the product of some second-hand formula. Instead, it is almost like a place you go. It's available to everyone, even though only a few venture into its territories. A desire to flourish rumbles in my gut just like it does in yours. "What if," writes author John Eldredge, "those deep desires in our hearts are telling us the truth, revealing to us the life we were *meant* to live?"[1]

What if flourishing was really just arriving at a place where I was at peace with myself and with others and my circumstances? What if flourishing was more a state of my heart than a ledger of my feats? What if to flourish meant

"THE MYSTERY OF HUMAN EXISTENCE LIES NOT JUST IN STAYING ALIVE BUT IN FINDING SOMETHING TO LIVE FOR."
—FYODOR DOSTOEVSKY

to live with every ounce of my being? What if it meant, as Thoreau said, to suck all the marrow out of life?

This book represents the best of what I've learned. It's a collection of lessons taught, wisdom gleaned, and truth revealed. It is not, however, a "how to" book, at least not in the traditional sense. There aren't "5 easy steps to the flourishing life," and there is no simple formula with a guaranteed outcome. If that's what you're looking for, you'll have to look elsewhere, but let me warn you—life just doesn't work that way. There is no flourishing template. What works well for one person might be a disaster for another. And, although it eludes many believers for their entire journey, God is not some automated dispenser that we direct with our inputs, where we insert our intent or activities and He responds with the suitable outcomes. That's just not how it works.

All I can offer are some principles that I've found to be true. It's up to you to figure out how the principles can be applied in your life. Before we go any further, though, I would like to spend a couple of chapters building a clear image of "what flourishing is." To do this, let's turn to one "mentor" who has helped me shape a correct understanding of flourishing. His name is Aristotle.

A LITTLE PHILOSOPHY GOES A LONG WAY

Flourishing, the Greek philosopher Aristotle said, is the innate potential of each individual to live a life of *enduring happiness, penetrating wisdom, optimal well-being,* and *authentic love and compassion.*[2] How's that for a 2,500-year-old street definition of flourishing? Let's look at those four ingredients.

When you think of happiness, what comes to mind?

Our western culture views happiness through a different lens than the ancient Greeks did. Where you and I might equate happiness with an emotion brought on by worldly pleasures, the Greeks defined happiness as a life well lived, a life focused on serving others, and a life contributing to the well-being of others. Happiness, to Aristotle and his band of brainiacs, was the *goal of life*. It was not something you attained via wealth, power, or status for one's own consumption.

You and I must deal with the contemporary lie that claims that in order to be happy we must do what we can to serve ourselves, to collect material possessions, to be successful in our chosen fields, and to gain wealth. Happiness is not these things. It is much more. It is something that can only be found when we look *beyond* ourselves to the needs and welfare of our fellow human beings.

Some years back I read a *Harvard Business Review* article titled "How Will You Measure Your Life?" by Clayton Christensen. He thoughtfully outlines the case for creating a strategy for life and folds his own life on top of the "model" for application. He ends the article by saying:

> "This past year I was diagnosed with cancer and faced the possibility that my life would end sooner than I'd planned. Thankfully, it now looks as if I will be spared. But the experience has given me important insight into my life. I have a pretty clear idea of how my ideas have generated enormous revenue for companies that have used my research: I know I've had a substantial impact. But as I've confronted this disease, it's been interesting to see how unimportant that impact is to me now. I've concluded that the metric by which God will assess my life isn't dollars

but individual people whose lives I have touched."[3]

Don't wait for an illness or a blow out to set the rule on the correct things to measure in life.

Another glaring difference between the ancients' view of flourishing and our view relates to time—specifically, immediacy versus longevity. While our focus tends to be immediate, theirs tended to be lasting. We think happiness can be grabbed now, as if we could pick it up on special at Macy's. But Aristotle attached the concept of *enduring* to *happiness.* He took the long view.

We can attain enduring happiness only when we extend our horizon. There we will survey our lives and either say we did what we could to help others, to live well and contribute to the good of all society *or* we will come face to face with the truth that selfish pursuits led us to a hollow ending, concluding regretfully, "If I only knew then what I know now."

It is impossible to flourish with a skewed view of happiness. Happiness is not just about us but also about others. It's not just about *the now* but also *the then.* Thought provoking, isn't it?

But that's just the beginning of Aristotle's life-altering perspective on flourishing.

Penetrating Wisdom

After happiness as a goal, in Aristotle's view, a life that flourishes must have wisdom as a guide. In our world of exponentially increasing information, we sometimes forget about the value of wisdom. But there's no flourishing without wise discernment and wise judgment. The ancients understood this better than we do.

In the Hebrew Old Testament we find a book of pithy one-liners full of general truth and advice. The book is called

Proverbs and was written by one of the wisest men to ever live: King Solomon.

Although Solomon also contributed to other "wisdom" books in the Old Testament, such as the enigmatic book called Ecclesiastes, he's best known for Proverbs. Solomon's reputation, wealth, and wisdom made him one of the most recognizable kings in the ancient Near East. When he spoke, it was worth listening to. His book of Proverbs begins like this:

> *These are the wise sayings of Solomon,*
> *David's son, Israel's king—*
> *Written down so we'll know how to live well and right,*
> *to understand what life means and where it's going;*
> *A manual for living,*
> *for learning what's right and just and fair;*
> *To teach the inexperienced the ropes*
> *and give our young people a grasp on reality.*
> *There's something here also for seasoned men and women,*
> *still a thing or two for the experienced to learn—*
> *Fresh wisdom to probe and penetrate,*
> *the rhymes and reasons of wise men and women.*
> – Proverbs 1:1-6 (MSG)

For Solomon, penetrating wisdom and well-being shimmered as the precious jewels of life. In the passage above, he reminds his reader how important wisdom is for the simple, the young, and the wise. But if you want to become wise, he cautions, you must pursue it. You must also be disciplined. Elsewhere in Proverbs, Solomon says, "Get wisdom!" It's a command.

But how?

How many of us have heard people say that wisdom comes from life experience and failing? Although there's some insight in that perspective, I disagree with its implied passivity. As a modern-day proverb states, "What the fool does in the end, the wise man does in the beginning."[4] Instead of just waiting to learn from the School of Hard Knocks, why not actively seek wisdom, and seek it as fast as we can?

Wisdom comes from hearing and heeding the wisdom that others speak or demonstrate. For example, we gain wisdom from a father, mother, friend, or co-worker who shares a recent failure. When they tell us what they learned, we have a choice. We can either regard their advice and thus procure wisdom, which saves us from the same failure, or we can ignore their counsel and follow the same path of misfortune.

What did you and I gain from disregarding the advice and insight of those who have gone before us? Certainly not wisdom! Maybe a headache, possibly a heartache, or even worse.

Wisdom allows us to flourish because it keeps us on the path. But be forewarned: It's not always an easy path. Wisdom does not promise ease. It promises fullness. It requires discipline and offers freedom.

And if we learn to value and to grow in wisdom, then we are ready to embrace the next element of flourishing.

Optimal Well-Being

Aristotle calls his third aspect of flourishing optimal well-being. This takes a little explanation, but when you understand his point, you realize he was right. This Greek philosopher says we don't need astounding success in one or two areas of life, with abysmal performance in other areas. That is, at best, unbalanced well-being. Instead, we need sustainable health and productivity across the whole terrain of what really matters in our lives. Optimal well-being, in other words.

Can you see how that's different from the way so many people live today?

After more than thirty years of executive coaching and the experience of my own victories and failures, I can tell you something with gritty confidence: One reason we fail to flourish is because we allow the true meaning of the word to be hijacked by a shallow substitute. We equate flourishing with selfish material acquisition—buying junk and thinking it will make us happy. We trade true wisdom for lax short-term thinking. And we allow immediate pleasures to rob us of deep, enduring love.

Aristotle's perspective forces us to rethink some assumptions and priorities. How can we flourish in a culture that never rests? A culture that says success equals the things you fill your house with or how much money you keep stashed in your bank account or what's parked in your garage? How can we flourish in a culture that says you must forsake the life-giving institution of family if you want a place at the corporate table? How can we flourish when we are running at breakneck speed from activity to activity and never tending to our soul?

Is it possible to thrive in our culture and not succumb to its interpretation of well-being? I say yes. But we have to make some pivots. Well-being is a soulish thing. It begins from the deep spaces within us and intermingles with the precious institutions of life: our relationships and personal worth, how we view others and ourselves and how we relate to our Maker. We will tackle this idea more completely in Chapter Four.

This brings us to the final and most relational aspect of Aristotle's definition of flourishing. And as usual, love sums it all up.

The love that Aristotle talks about is not a mere emotion. It's a way of life. Love as a word sounds nice and reads well in a letter or a greeting card, but it means nothing unless followed by definitive action. If your girlfriend or husband says, "I love you," but then treats you with disdain, will you remember their words of devotion and love? No.

If, however, I say that I love my wife and I build my schedule in a way that honors her and honors the time needed for us to continue in a thriving relationship, then my words match my action. And it's not just any action; love and compassion are defined by sacrifice. Like the wise sage Olaf the Snowman said in *Frozen*, "Love is putting someone else's needs before yours.… Some people are worth melting for."

On a more serious note, Jesus of Nazareth said, "*Greater love has no one than this: to lay down one's life for one's friends*" (*John 15:13 NIV*). How deeply we love will be reflected in how much we sacrifice for the well-being of someone else. As the Apostle John states, "*Let us not love with words or speech but with actions and in truth*" (*1 John 3:18 NIV*).

THE IMPORTANCE OF THOUGHTS

What it means to *flourish*, I'm convinced, needs a reset. Aristotle is just one help in doing this. The greatest thinkers agree that flourishing means to live life to the fullest in an authentic and sustainable way. This requires that we strip away the veneer of culture and get a bit dirty with honesty. A reset demands that we challenge our current way of thinking. My friend and best-selling author John C. Maxwell says that "stinking thinking" can ruin us. How we think affects how we act.

If we continue to gauge flourishing in terms of the quantity of things we accumulate rather than by the quality of relationships we establish—the depth at which we love and allow ourselves to be loved—and the amount of good we initiate, then we'll never experience the beauty of what it feels like to fully blossom. On the other hand, if we can work for enduring happiness, seek optimal well-being, discipline ourselves to get wisdom, and walk in love, we will truly flourish.

Life is meant to be more than just enduring our way to the end. It's not about surviving; it's about thriving. It's not about settling; it's about surpassing. We're not supposed to be a spindly sapling that never grows and blossoms; we're supposed to be like a majestic maple, digging in our roots, spreading our branches, and being a blessing to anyone who comes near. We're supposed to flourish.

But we can miss it. Can't we?

That's why, over the next several chapters, I'm going to be describing some of the practices, disciplines, and mental shifts that you can take to go from merely existing to flourishing. They may be surprising to you. They may seem countercultural and counterintuitive. But given that most people lead lives of merely existing, don't you think flourishing takes an approach to life that is out of the ordinary?

I invite you to give these practices a chance. See if they don't give you a life that's different from what you've grown accustomed to—but feels much more like what you were meant for all along.

Flourishing is what God always intended.

"I CAME SO THEY CAN HAVE
REAL AND ETERNAL LIFE,
MORE AND BETTER LIFE THAN
THEY EVER DREAMED OF."
— JOHN 10:10 (MSG)

CHAPTER 2

THE TRUTH ABOUT PROSPERITY

*Redefine Around
Shalom*

"Not everything that counts can be counted and not all that is counted really counts." – William Cameron Bruce, a 1960s sociologist

IT WAS THE day before Christmas, and I had run to the store for a few last minute groceries. I don't remember exactly what was on my list but I imagine we were missing a couple of items to round out our traditional Christmas breakfast. I was moving quickly through the fruit section and ran straight into my friend Jim. Before I could even say hi, Jim pressed into my space too closely, and asked, "Hey, can we talk for a minute?" I said, "Sure, but it is Christmas Eve and I need to get home soon. How about next week or even the following week?" He leaned in even closer and asked, "Can we talk now?" So we moved over into the corner of a very large and busy grocery store and he started unloading.

Jim had been a friend for years. He was a good businessman and seemed to be the perfect picture of prosperity.

He was the guy hosting massive parties whenever the calendar offered a conceivable reason. He was the one jetting off to the Caribbean whenever he felt his sunbaked tan was losing its sheen. He was the one living large with all looking on in envious wonder. Family. Kids. Business. Houses. Toys. Power. Smiles. He was living well…or so we all thought.

In that busy grocery store corner, though, Jim revealed a much different reality. He confessed that his life was a disastrous wreck. He was facing lawsuits, and he had already lost his family and his businesses. He had no money and even fewer friends. A life normally overflowing with abundance was empty.

I drove home stunned.

"Somewhere along the way, Steve, I lost my way. I fell off balance. My formula for life and success has utterly failed me and I am a wreck."

A picture of prosperity to a desperate wreck! How does that happen? How does someone who seems to be doing so well end up as financially, emotionally, and relationally broke as Jim? The truth is, more often than not folks end up like Jim because they have been bankrupt for quite some time; it just takes a while for the accounting to catch up.

Like too many of us, Jim equated a flourishing life with worldly success and was left with a lopsided and empty understanding of prosperity. Even though it looked like Jim's life was a towering and impressive structure, it was really nothing more than a deceptive façade, entirely lacking a foundation and resting precariously on a ledge. Unfortunately, this warped notion of prosperity, which makes financial and material success the alone ultimate, can't fulfill. Just as it did for my friend, it can lead us to skewed and incomplete lives in which we chase a mere fraction of the true prosperity available. As Christians, we are called to so much more. We are called to true prosperity.

WHAT IS PROSPERITY, ANYWAY?

When I look up the word *prosperity* in the dictionary, I find it defined as "a state of being *prosperous*." Well, that's not very helpful. What does prosperous mean? The Latin meaning behind the word *prosperous* defines it a little bit better: "doing well."

So, if I'm prosperous then I'm doing well. But the question still remains—doing well in what? Work? Family? My health? Is prosperity something that can be segmented and walled off? Can we be prosperous in one area, while floundering

"THE TRUTH IS, MORE OFTEN THAN NOT FOLKS END UP LIKE JIM BECAUSE THEY HAVE BEEN BANKRUPT FOR QUITE SOME TIME; IT JUST TAKES A WHILE FOR THE ACCOUNTING TO CATCH UP."

in another? Or, does the very idea of prosperity require a complete and integrated view of our lives?

If we dig a bit deeper, we find that prosperity is an all-encompassing concept. Look at Jeremiah 29:7 in the Old Testament. In this Scripture passage, God is instructing the Israelites on how to live as exiles in Babylon. He tells them:

"Seek the peace and prosperity of the city to which I have carried you into exile. Pray to the Lord for it, because if it prospers, you too will prosper" (NIV).

What is God telling the Israelites to pray for as exiles? The Hebrew word for prosperity here is *shalom*, and it means "peace, soundness, or completeness." The idea of *shalom* is far from our modern ideas of prosperity. Though *shalom* can also mean welfare relating to happiness and fortune, it is never a welfare without wholeness. The history of Israel, after all, was littered with kings who had plenty of "stuff" but little shalom. My buddy Jim certainly found wealth, but it was welfare or prosperity without wholeness or completeness. No shalom. No true prosperity.

A PROSPERITY GOSPEL

I believe in a prosperity gospel, but not the kind you're thinking about. In today's Christian landscape there are myriad views on the so-called "Prosperity Gospel." A quick click through early morning television will give you all the examples you care to find. Some folks blast such a view of the gospel as a crass and materialistic interpretation where a person can claim what they want and basically employ the Holy Spirit to do their bidding with regard to "good fortunes." Others view such prosperity as the very social construct we were called to live within. God blesses those who bless others, they would say.

For me, I fall in the *radical middle*. I don't believe God calls His children to live expectant of great riches in terms of material gain. But I also don't think money and good health are inherently bad. We all pray for blessing and good health for our children and those we love. We also see great men and women of God each day who use their great fortunes to make the world a better place; who help those less fortunate, who inspire entrepreneurs with encouragement and resources to educate young children in Africa, to provide opportunity for the destitute in New York City, and the list goes on.

But it's not enough to simply be in the middle. You have to have a more robust definition of prosperity. I've reframed the "Prosperity Gospel" as the *Shalom* Gospel. I believe God is a good God and desires us to flourish. He blesses each of us with experience and opportunity that He expects to be used for His glory and honor. He wants us to utilize prosperous circumstances in order that we might bring blessing to all. We are to seek peace and wholeness for ourselves and for others. When we do that, when we seek prosperity in our own contexts, we are living out a dynamic and whole gospel.

WHAT IS YOUR TREASURE?

The real issue, then, for those following a "name it, claim it" kind of faith isn't that they are asking for too much, but rather that they are asking for too little. They've decided that prosperity can *only* look a certain way, and because of that, they've missed out on a much more abundant, complete offering. As C.S. Lewis so eloquently describes it, they have been "far too easily pleased":

> "It would seem that Our Lord finds our desires not too strong, but too weak. We are half-hearted creatures, fooling about with drink and sex and ambition when

infinite joy is offered to us, like an ignorant child who wants to go on making mud pies in a slum because he cannot imagine what is meant by the offer of a holiday at the sea."[5]

This sad state that Lewis describes is precisely where we can all end up, when we pursue a shallow version of prosperity. To use the words of Jesus, when we treasure things of this world, our hearts end up there as well. So, if you run after worldly prosperity, then it's a safe bet that your heart may feel right at home counting your money and making your mud pies. Again, it's not that money and possessions are inherently bad; it's when our heart becomes wrapped around and consumed by the mud pies of material gain, selfish ambition, and personal privilege that we get in trouble.

It's our motives that knock us off course.

The Apostle Paul says: *"For am I now seeking the approval of man, or of God? Or am I trying to please man? If I were still trying to please man, I would not be a servant of Christ"* (Galatians 1:10 ESV). This verse asks the right question. Who am I trying to please? With regard to our discussion here, we could ask, "Why am I striving so fiercely after worldly prosperity?"

With perhaps even greater force, James likewise brutally confronts us with questions of motivation, demanding we take a long, honest look at ourselves. This verse from the book of James is probably the toughest one to stomach:

"What causes quarrels and what causes fights among you? Is it not this, that your passions are at war within you? You desire and do not have, so you murder. You covet and cannot obtain, so you fight and quarrel. You do not have, because you do not ask. You ask and do not receive, because you ask wrongly, to spend it on your passions. You adulterous people! Do you not know that

"NO ONE IS BORN A NARCISSIST...THEY ARE DEVELOPED."

friendship with the world is enmity with God? Therefore whoever wishes to be a friend of the world makes himself an enemy of God. Or do you suppose it is to no purpose that the Scripture says, 'He yearns jealously over the spirit that he has made to dwell in us'?" (*James 4:1-5 ESV*).

Ouch! I don't know about you, but the term *adulterous* is not one I'd ever like to be saddled with. James doesn't beat around the bush. He cuts right to the heart of the issue. Our desires aren't fulfilled and prosperity remains elusive because we love the world more than we love God. I, for one, don't want to be an enemy of God. I want my motives to be driven by His ambitions for my life and this world, not my own.

When left to myself, a selfish ambition can take over and control my life. No one is born a narcissist…they are developed. But when I'm submitted to God, my heart becomes like *His* and my ambitions become like *His*.

Who knows why your friend Sarah received the blessing of a new home on the golf course? Who knows why your friend John received a promotion and you haven't received one in years? We're responsible for our own motives, our own ambitions.

SEEKING CONTENTMENT

The flourishing life is the life that rests in contentment. Remember that passage in Jeremiah we looked at earlier? Think about what God is *really* asking the Israelites to do. He's saying, "Hey, I know you're in exile. But don't mope around and feel sorry for yourself. Get out there and make friends with your captors. Help them. Seek peace and wholeness for their nation. Serve them in a way that astounds them. Be content with where I have you and see what blessings come of it."

In short, God is suggesting that the Israelites seek contentment, regardless of what their circumstances might be. Just think, if you can be content while living in exile then you should be able to do well when you get back to your own country.

More and more I talk to folks from all walks of life that are burning the candle at both ends trying to get ahead. They strive and worry and stress, and for what? Sure, my northwest Arkansas demeanor is a bit more laid back than most. What can I say? The Ozarks have been good to me! But seriously, it has taken me years to understand the magic to living a contented life. It's trust. For such a little word, it really packs a wallop!

I give my endeavors to God. I open my hands, with my ambitions exposed and say, "Okay God, here it is. This thing or issue is Yours. I'm going to do my best to get it done, but I'm counting on You to keep me in check. I trust You to make it happen."

I've talked to CEOs of thriving companies who can't ever take a Sabbath rest because they fear falling behind. Behind? Behind in what? What race is perpetually going on in this life? Am I missing something? Often they can't relax and rest because they don't trust the success of their efforts to anyone but themselves.

As if God couldn't shut down our endeavors at anytime, we think we need to run ourselves into the ground to keep it all afloat.

I love how pastor Eugene Peterson paraphrases Philippians 4:12: *"I've learned by now to be quite content whatever my circumstances. I'm just as happy with little as with much, with much as with little. I've found the recipe for being happy whether full or hungry, hands full or hands empty. Whatever I have, wherever I am, I can make it through anything in the One who makes me who I am"* (MSG).

Yes! Ultimate trust in God in whatever my circumstances. That's my goal. I want to trust God with everything so that my circumstances don't dictate my state of being. I don't want to respond harshly to my wife and children because I'm not "making it" as the world defines it. I don't want to get caught judging my self-worth by a worldly standard that says I have to get, get, get, and get some more to be prosperous. I don't want my motives and ambitions to be hijacked for bad.

My flourishing in this life is a direct result of how well or how little I trust God. If I can grab hold of the power of contentment and live in that sweet spot of life, then I'm good. It is there that I find real Shalom and prosperity. It really has nothing to do with my northwest Arkansas demeanor. I've simply learned, through failures and victories, that flourishing has nothing to do with worldly prosperity and everything to do with living with my hands open and saying, "Okay, God, this thing is Yours. Come what may, I give it all to You. I'm happy just being Your kid. Let's roll!"

"MAY THE LORD BLESS YOU AND PROTECT YOU. MAY THE LORD SMILE ON YOU AND BE GRACIOUS TO YOU. MAY THE LORD SHOW YOU HIS FAVOR AND GIVE YOU HIS *[SHALOM]*."

–NUMBERS 6:24-26 (NLT)

CHAPTER 3

STRONG VOICE

*Get Comfortable but not Addicted
to Your Own Sound*

"Insist on yourself; never imitate. Your own gift you can present every moment with the cumulative force of a whole life's cultivation; but of the adopted talent of another, you have only an extemporaneous, half possession. That which each can do best, none but his Maker can teach him."
– Ralph Waldo Emerson

IN THE MOVIE *Ray*, there's a scene where Ray Charles's record producer, Ahmet Ertegun, challenges his protégé. "Ray," he says, "I want to tell you something and I don't want you to take it wrong."

"Then give it to me straight."

"I signed you because I sensed something special in you, not because you sound like Nat King Cole or Charles Brown."

"I thought you like what I do," Ray replies.

"We … we love the timbre of your voice, we like your virtuosity, your energy …"

"But not my music …"

"C'mon man, I didn't say that."

"Ahmet, this is what I do, man. I gotta make a living. This is what people want. I don't know no other way."

"We gotta help you find one."

The incomparable Ray Charles, the accomplished singer and songwriter, the dynamic performer, was told to find his own voice. Not the pitch or the tone of his voice, but rather the substance behind it. He had all the tools a singer needed to make a living, but he hadn't yet caught hold of the one thing that would set him apart: *his unique signature*. To this point, he was simply a talented copy. He didn't know who he really was. Once he figured that out, once he found his voice, that's when something really special happened.

Your voice is not just the sound coming out of your mouth. It's the signature coming out of your life. It is that unique sound emerging from the chorus of life messages within you. It is the singular music that resonates forth as you operate within your created and discovered giftedness. It is the discovery of that which is distinctly me, or in your case, distinctly you. Having a job, getting a paycheck, or even succeeding, though, doesn't necessarily mean we have found our voice.

One of my mentors and teachers, the late Howard Hendricks, often said, "All people are born original, but most people die a copy." When I consider what it means to be "born original," I think of the uniqueness that is woven into each of God's creations. I think of my createdness. I was born with a certain skillset. I'm good at things that you're not good at. You can do things I could never dream of doing. The ancients referred to this uniqueness as our *vocatio*, what many folks today refer to as "calling." You and I are geared for something specific. Like an intricately constructed timepiece, we are built with a series of gears that run perfectly when in sync. Some of us possess a wide range of gears. Others of us possess only a few or even one. The amount doesn't matter. What matters is that we realize that we were created with a purpose and were given the tools to carry out that purpose.

Unfortunately, many of us make decisions about our life and work based on what other people tell us about our voice, about how it should sound, and how we should use it. Because of this, we tend to choose *careers*, rather than *callings*. Putting aside what we know we were made for, we opt for stability and comfort over God-given passions and wiring. We say, "It's just not practical," or "I'll do that when I retire." All the while, we suppress our unique voice until it's so quiet that we hardly hear it, or even recognize it ourselves.

Why? Why do we so willingly lay aside something as profoundly important as our calling, and instead pick up something as common as a career? At least in part, it is because we have constructed a false dichotomy between the two. We've said, "You can follow your passions and do what you were made for, or you can be prudent, find a steady job and take care of your responsibilities. Prudent or Passionate. One or the other. You can't have your cake and eat it too."

To that I say, "Why not?" Why can't we be practically minded good stewards, and yet still honor our calling? Even if your current job doesn't perfectly line up with your voice, that's no excuse to ignore it.

Consider my friend Kyle. Not too long ago, Kyle spent several years working in a print shop. He knew he needed the job, but he also knew he was meant for something specific. So the whole time he worked in the print shop, he also free-lanced as a writer. He worked hard at his career, and equally hard at his *vocatio*. Today, he's a published writer.

My point here is that my friend didn't let someone wedge him into a career that he wasn't suited for. He dove deep into his createdness, his *vocatio*, and developed a strong voice. He's an original not because he's the only writer in the world, but because he's found his unique voice in a career he was created to do.

GROWING BEYOND KARAOKE

When I look at the Christian leadership landscape, I see men and women leading from the strength of their unique voice. But I also see, in growing numbers, folks who see the success of other leaders and pattern their own leadership and voice after them. We see ministry success or professional success or even family success, and we immediately believe they've unlocked the secret.

Authentic Christian leadership, however, must stem from an individual's uniqueness. This isn't just a quaint axiom; it's a biblical idea. When God formed you and I in our mother's wombs, He did so with a specific plan. Do you think God would make a plan for you and not equip you for it? When we read David's poem, otherwise known as Psalm 139, we discover a God who doesn't just make carbon copies from a template. Rather, we find a God who personally weaves each one of us with care and wisdom.

> *You have searched me,* Lord, *and you know me. …*
> *For you created my inmost being; you knit me together*
> *in my mother's womb (Psalm 139:1, 13 NIV).*

If King David was right, if God took such tremendous care in crafting the unique wiring of each of us, shouldn't we take just as much care in how we make use of that uniqueness? Before we do that, though, we have to understand: "You are the only you God made. …God made you and broke the mold," says Max Lucado.

So, what's your life signature? What's your unique voice among a sea of voices all clamoring to be heard?

If you aren't sure, it's easy to be overwhelmed and even confused by the idea of developing a unique voice. In reality, however, it's just about discovering the original life we were intended to live. This does not require a mystical experience. It simply requires you to turn around, look at your life, and evaluate the road you've traveled thus far. What makes your heart jump? What do you find pleasure in doing? What specific tools has God equipped you with? Where do you seem to thrive?

When we finally step into the answers to these questions,

"TRUE HUMILITY ISN'T
THINKING LESS OF
YOURSELF; IT IS THINKING
OF YOURSELF LESS."
– C.S. LEWIS

---

we find our voice. And when we do, the confusion and the blur reorganize and clarify. When I personally began to understand my unique signature, I began to see things differently. For one thing, I began to understand competition in a more healthy way, no longer seeing it as a vindictive play to put someone else down so I could get ahead. Finding your voice also helps with real humility. Richard Foster, the wise pastor and theologian, in his book *Prayer*, says that to live with a humble heart means to live with eyes that see truth: truth about yourself, truth about others, and truth about the context you're in.[6] C.S. Lewis adds, "True humility isn't thinking less of yourself; it is thinking of yourself less."[7]

When I understand the truth about myself, I see myself as God sees me. This gives me supreme confidence in my identity. Likewise, when I understand the truth about others, I see them through God's eyes as well. Seeing these two truths gives me the ability to discern—I can see people in their createdness (how God sees them) and I'm not threatened by their work, projects, or status. When I understand the truth about my context, I see life as an opportunity to honor God and serve others in every situation. Humility, you see, does not mean that we roll around in the mud pretending as if we are completely bereft of any talents or worth. It is not about having a low opinion of yourself and a high opinion of others. That is, at best, false humility. True humility is having a right opinion of both parties, and most importantly, of God. Again, C.S. Lewis captured this desired state wonderfully in his classic work, *The Screwtape Letters*:

> [God] wants to bring the man to a state of mind in
> which he could design the best cathedral in the world,
> and know it to be the best, and rejoice in the fact, without
> being any more (or less) or otherwise glad at having done

it than he would be if it had been done by another. [God] wants him, in the end, to be so free from any bias in his own favor that he can rejoice in his own talents as frankly and gratefully as in his neighbor's talents – or in a sunrise, an elephant, or a waterfall. He wants each man, in the long run, to be able to recognize all creatures (even himself) as glorious and excellent things.[8]

In short, humility demands that we see the world with wide-open eyes; that I serve others from a state of confidence in my own identity.

Additionally, when I began to understand my unique voice, ambition finally made sense to me. Rather than a misguided pursuit of self, ambition became a desire tied up in my *createdness* and in my relationship with Christ. When Paul uses the concept of "ambition" in the New Testament he is referring to the less noble version, and he does so in a clearly negative way. Does this mean that ambition is always a bad thing? I don't think it does. Paul's use of *selfish ambition*—in verses like 2 Corinthians 12:20, Galatians 5:20, Philippians 2:3, and others—however, is an important corrective and helps keep ambition in its proper place. Paul defines selfish ambition as "empty glory," and equates it with vain conceit. While ambition can be motivated by the very strong human desire for glory, Paul warns that such glory is empty when we strive after it to satisfy our own desires.

In contrast to this selfish ambition are those desires that are correctly oriented. When I take on a new project or business venture and God remains at the center of my vision, establishing and guiding my ethics and my ultimate goal for that particular venture, then ambition starts feeling like a God-thing instead of a Steve-thing because it begins in and is rooted in my relationship with Him.

I think that people often miss the idea of uniqueness. They think that to be unique you need to differentiate yourself from the pack, that you need to make some kind of big splash in your industry, that you need to get a great degree from a top tier school. But that stuff is all just window dressing. Being unique is really about discovering and remaining true to the person God created you to be. Sometimes we all need to be reminded of our createdness. It's easy to drift from that center and when that happens, it's a tough journey back. But the beauty of being a child of God is that even that hard journey can be part of cultivating your unique strong voice.

AGAINST THE CURRENT

So, what next? Once we discover and begin living in the confidence of our unique voices we will inevitably look for direction. We will feel pressure to utilize our voices, to pick a direction and run full-steam ahead. This can be dangerous. As we consider these directions, I am reminded that all the great leaders might have to swim against the current for a bit.

It's not necessarily a rule of thumb. By that I mean you shouldn't automatically seek to be the contrarian and always swim against the current just to be *that* guy or gal. You should, however, be willing to turn left when everyone else turns right if you know that to be the direction your voice will find the most resonance.

Be warned, though, our culture operates better when you swim *with* the current.

Step back in time with me for a moment. I want to revisit a story most of us know and love, the story of David and Goliath. Among other things, it's a story of someone who swam against the current.

You might remember that David was visiting the front lines of battle in order to deliver food to his brothers. When he arrives, he sees a spectacle that makes his blood boil and confuses him. He doesn't understand why no one has taken out the enemy warrior Goliath.

"What will be done for the man who kills this Philistine and removes this disgrace from Israel?" David asked. *"Who is this uncircumcised Philistine that he should defy the armies of the living God?" (1 Samuel 17:26 NIV).*

Interestingly, David asks twice about the bounty given to the person who defeats Goliath. Sometimes, extraordinary circumstances can motivate us and reveal our unique voice. David confirms the bounty again and word gets to King Saul. Once David is before the king he says, *"Let no one lose heart on account of this Philistine; your servant will go and fight him" (1 Samuel 17:32 NIV).*

King Saul doubts David, but finally allows him to fight Goliath. The next step is crucial in understanding the concept of voice. The king orders his servants to outfit David with his own (Saul's) heavy armor—what Saul believes is suitable and conventional for killing giants. But David can hardly stand up while wearing all that gear. Keep in mind: David is no slouch. David is a young stud who's killed both bear and lion while defending his father's sheep.

But the culture said, "Look, if you're going to be a giant killer this is what you must wear." David, on the other hand, says, "This is not how *I* kill giants. I kill them the way I kill bears and lions." With good intentions, the king was prescribing David's signature and voice.

David takes off the gear, picks up his slingshot, and slays the giant. The accolades of David's accomplishment followed him all the days of his life. He won in the garb of his own voice and signature. Likewise, sometimes in life we must be willing to confront situations in a way that goes against common convention and standard operating procedure.

Slaying a giant was no small feat. Most warriors would have been grateful for Saul's gift of weaponry. David, however, knew who he was, and he was confident in his own gifts because he had tested them. He was also confident in God. David had forged his identity in the quiet wilderness, watching sheep. His experience with the bear and the lion gave him confidence to approach Goliath with trust in God and trust in his own "unique voice." He was a shepherd, adept with the sling and fearless with his hands. It made sense to kill the giant in his own fashion, not in the fashion so common to the culture.

Be careful, though, not to fall into the trap of the rebellious spirit. David's example to us does not empower us to be unruly and independent all our lives, to be rebels just for the sake of being rebels. We won't always have to take a radically different approach to solving problems or discovering our voice. Life's not a big four-wheel Jeep expedition void of rules. Just like there's a time and a place to set the generic giant-killing armor aside, pick up our sling, and take out the giant on our own terms, there is also a time and a place for imitating those who've mentored and guided us. Paul hints to this in Hebrews 13:7—"*Remember your leaders, who spoke the word of God to you. Consider the outcome of their way of life and imitate their faith*" (NIV), and in 1 Corinthians 11:1—"*Imitate me, as I do the Messiah*" (ISV).

"YES, WE MUST DISCOVER AND OPERATE IN OUR UNIQUE VOICE. BUT WE MUST BE CAREFUL NOT TO BECOME ADDICTED TO OUR OWN VOICE."

THE DANGEROUS SIDE OF VOICE

I mentioned earlier how too often we're content to mimic others instead of honing our own voice. We readily take on the persona and styling of our favorite authors, speakers, leaders, and pastors. I believe that when we do this, we become less of ourselves. If the only ideas or rhetoric we convey is simply a copy of someone else's book or blog, then we haven't really found our voice—we're just copying theirs.

My real voice is tied to who I am, what I do, where I've been, what I am passionate about, how I want to influence others, my calling, my dreams, my talents, my skills, my experience, my education, my ambitions, and my innate wiring. It takes us a lifetime to become authentic in all the nuances of this, but the sooner we forget about mimicking other voices and begin cultivating our own, the sooner we find fulfillment.

But the confidence we find in our own voice can also turn into a hazardous pitfall. Yes, we must discover and operate in our unique voice. But we must be careful not to become addicted to our own voice. When we become addicted to our own voice, for example, we develop blind spots because we're listening to the voice of one. When we operate in blind spots it's easy to become arrogant and stubborn because our own voice, our own narrative, is the only one we see or value. Someone addicted to their own voice has no pure energy or appetite for anyone else. All story lines and conversation flows from and to the voice-addicted person. It is exhilarating and powerful to find my own voice but I must be careful. It can't become an end in itself. Although the flourishing life is yoked to someone discovering their own voice, that life will wither if our own voice becomes so loud and dominating that all other voices have no sound and beauty. Just like we can spot someone who has never found their voice and is living life on someone else's sound, we can also easily spot the person who has become addicted to their own voice.

John the Baptist is an excellent positive example in this regard. John the Baptist could easily fit into my hometown culture of northwest Arkansas. With his burly beard, nappy hair, and love of rivers he'd quickly find a home at an angler's cabin, just hanging out with the boys. John was indeed a radical figure in the New Testament, and, to me, stands as a great example of a person who did not confuse his voice with the Master's face.

When people heard John preach they were amazed and drawn to him. He had discovered his voice, and it was powerful and convincing. But he was quick to remind those who wanted to elevate him that he was just a voice, that he was just paving the way for the true Messiah. John knew the difference in voice and face. He kept things in perspective— he used his gifts with confidence and freedom *but* he always pointed to Jesus when given undue praise.

In today's world of leadership platform building, it's increasingly difficult to remain grounded. We're told to develop our voice. We're told to cultivate a personal brand. We are told it is all about building our platform—more views, more likes, more traffic, more exposure, more "us." We're encouraged to develop our stories as if we're the lead character in a novel. But John's got some news for us. This story is not about you and it's not about me. It's about Jesus. When given the chance, will we quickly point to Jesus as the author of our gifts and the giver of our blessings? Or will we allow the accolades and accomplishments to create blind spots for our egos?

Here is where the humility that we discussed before helps. You and I will be less apt to become addicted to our own voices if we cling to the truth of our createdness, to a heavenly humility. If we want to flourish in our calling and not get addicted to our voice we will:

Maintain a healthy understanding of our place before God.

Realize that life is not about "me."

Recognize that my skill and voice contribute to the choir of life. But this ain't no solo concert.

Be comfortable sharing the stage with others, promoting others.

THEY ARE LIKE TREES
PLANTED ALONG THE
RIVERBANK, BEARING FRUIT
EACH SEASON. THEIR LEAVES
NEVER WITHER, AND THEY
PROSPER IN ALL THEY DO.
— PSALM 1:3 (NLT)

CHAPTER 4

THE SCHIZOPHRENIC YOU

*Use a Composite
Scorecard to Win*

"God gave me a message to deliver and a horse to ride. I rode the horse to death and can no longer deliver the message." – Robert Murray McCheyne, Presbyterian preacher, 1827

I WANT TO tell you about a friend of mine. Maybe you know him.

Joe owns his own business. He works 60-70 hours a week, always setting the standard with his enthusiasm and leadership. His employees love him and regularly tell him how much he inspires them.

Exercise

Joe gets up every morning at 5:00 a.m. and exercises for 60 minutes. He also goes to the local wellness co-op to pick up his meals, which are prepared daily by a special nutritionist. He takes vitamins and supplements, and his wife squeezes fresh juices for him daily. And, naturally, he only drinks purified store-bought water—nothing but the healthy stuff for Joe.

Family

At the breakfast table every morning, Joe enjoys visiting with his wife and kids as they casually talk about what the upcoming day holds. He carefully seizes every teachable moment with his kids and never misses a chance to stir in wisdom from his heritage and life.

It is his responsibility and joy to drop the kids off at school every day and at least once every two weeks he goes to school to eat with his kids. Joe promptly walks through the door every day at 5:00 p.m. at which time he changes clothes and immediately begins to play with his kids followed by fatherly assistance on each child's homework. He is especially good at math, science, English, history, philosophy, and all things computer.

Every night Joe spends quality time with each of his *seven* children before he tucks them into bed with homespun stories and prayers. He and Sally enjoy a date every Tuesday night without exception. And Sally has been known to tell her supper club that Joe is the most romantic, sexy man on the planet.

Every weekend is a family blowout: camping, hiking, a visit to the museum, and even clean-up time at the house is an exciting adventure when Joe's leading the way. The neighbors idolize Joe—and rightly so. Joe cuts his grass every weekend according to the groundskeeper's manual for Augusta National Golf Club—his yard stripes are perfect. You will not find a better family man than Joe.

Church

Joe and his family never miss church. He teaches a community group, is adult sponsor of a junior high cell group, is on the finance committee, and was recently asked to be an elder. Not a year has gone by in the last 25 years that Joe has not read the Bible completely through, and not a Sunday goes by that Joe and his wife don't have a special guest with them during the service.

Community

Joe recently completed his commitment as chairman of the local United Way campaign, but he has agreed to act as interim until they find an adequate replacement. No one else quite feels up to the job, especially since Joe set new records every single year. This past year they raised $2.7 million. There are even rumors that he could be asked to join the National Committee, which he would obviously have to take. What an opportunity! How could he pass that up?

Joe might be the single-most compassionate person in town. He visits the homeless woods every weekend taking food and necessities, and at least once a month helps move an abandoned child into a local Safe Family.

Good old, give back, *community* Joe!

Leisure

No one will ever accuse Joe of going too fast and pushing too hard. He ties his own flies and has a list of the top 100 spots in the world to hook a trophy trout. He has 27 down and 73 to go. He is an expert marksman, plays chess, and is one salty golfer.

He also keeps a stack of Sudoku magazines next to his bed for "productive relaxation." Speaking of bed, if there is one guy that you can count on to get a good night's sleep every night, it's Joe—8-9 hours without fail. None of that going in to work every morning dragging! Joe is relaxed. High blood pressure is not going to ever happen with easy-going Joe.

BACK TO REALITY

If you haven't figured it out by now, Joe does not exist. How could he? The math alone will never add up. We might be able to mirror Joe's life in one or two phases, but never across the board. It just isn't possible. This entire parody reminds me of the man-made marketing concoction created by a group of beach buddies back in the late 90s that has grown to a $300 million dollar worldwide brand called Tommy Bahama.[9] There is no real Tommy Bahama and there is no real Super Joe. So why would any one of us aspire to be "Super Joe" if we know he is just a man-made promotional fiction? And further, why would we listen to folks—and there are many in our culture—who want to line up Super Joe as our ideal?

One part of the answer is simple. Inside every one of us is an inherent knowledge that we are meant to do more than one thing. To be effective, we know that we need to juggle at least a few balls all at once. At the same time, a perhaps even stronger impulse tells us that we need to do those things well. So, even though we know Super Joe doesn't exist, we feel an internal (and likely external) call to effectively manage a never-ending portfolio of tasks, opportunities, relationships, and dreams. This can be an overwhelming proposition, no matter what your ideal is. When that ideal is some version of "Super Joe," life quickly becomes an exhausting, emptying treadmill.

To drive this point home, a world-class counselor friend of mine often gives a particular homework assignment to the hyper-achieving, Super Joe's who walk into his office. He tells them to buy a hamster wheel and put it on the desk in their office. It is an ever-present reminder that the chase is futile.

We must learn to manage ourselves well and be comfortable with the fact that "I'm not going to be Super Joe, but I am going to be a great portfolio manager." I can be me—the composite, multifaceted me that God created, and I can do so with confidence and no regrets.

CHASE A COMPOSITE SCORECARD

So how do we stay centered and full of peace, all while ambitiously living a multifaceted life and not falling prey to the inherent stresses that go along with it? It begins by giving up the Super-Joe chase, and instead, chasing a strong composite scorecard.

"WE WERE CREATED BY GOD
WITH NOT ONE, BUT SEVERAL
VOCATIOS—SEVERAL
CALLINGS OR VOCATIONS."

When I use the term *scorecard*, I am referring to a "grade" that we can assign to the various aspects of our life. And when I use the term *composite*, I'm talking about the collection of crucial assignments in your world. Joe's areas of scoring were work, exercise, family, church, community, and leisure. Let's stick with these since we're all familiar with them and they meet us where we are each day.

I also want to revisit one of the main concepts in the "Strong Voice" chapter—our unique "wiredness." If you remember, this uniqueness is what many today refer to as calling. The concept comes from the Latin word *vocatio*, from which we get our word *vocation*. Our vocation is the thing we were created to do or the thing we are "summoned to."

While the idea of a unique calling is fairly common, I think we need to expand it. In order to live at ease as multifaceted people, balancing several things at once, there is something that we must attempt to understand. Here it is: We were created by God with not one, but several *vocatios*—several callings or vocations. We have been "summoned by our Maker" to effectively engage a number of assignments all at the same time. If this is true, I think it is also fair to assume that at least some part of our unique wiring is specifically tuned with this multifaceted aim in mind.

OUR MANY VOCATIOS

You and I each possess a *vocatio* tied closely to our natural skills and abilities. Many times this is that special thing that you were drawn to or showed an aptitude for when you were young; it came easy to you and you loved to do it. My friend Tim, who helped with this book, is gifted with words. Tim also used to own a landscape company and excelled at that profession for a number of years. Tim enjoys landscape work, and could have very easily pursued that as a career path. His ability to landscape, however, does not negate the fact that Tim is uniquely wired for a specific occupation. His *vocation* is "writer."

What this means is that we can all choose various career paths and those may or may not align with our *vocatio*. You may choose medicine because you want to make money and have security. Or perhaps you go into sales because it provides the clearest path for advancement. That's all fine, but what about that special giftedness for architecture and design? Do you see what I'm getting at? You have been created with a certain *vocatio* and the occupation you choose may or may not line up with that. When they do meet, though, that is when you discover your sweet spot in life.

So, your first vocation has to do with your skills as a person—skills that play into your occupation.

But you also have been given a *vocatio* within the institution of the family. If you are a woman reading this, and you are married with a child on the way, your family *vocatio* is "Mother and Wife." This is a beautiful and essential vocation, and there are certain responsibilities that go along with those roles. Likewise for men reading this, if you are married and have children, then your family *vocatio* is "Father and Husband." Certain responsibilities accompany these roles. That is a calling and a summons.

You also have a *vocatio* as "child of God," or the temple of God. It is up to you to act as a faithful steward of the body God's given you. While you live out all of these other vocations, you must also care for your body, remembering it needs rest and relaxation.

Finally, you have a community *vocatio* and are compelled to work for the prosperity of your local community. How you

"HAPPINESS IS NOT A
MATTER OF INTENSITY
BUT OF BALANCE, ORDER,
RHYTHM AND HARMONY."
– THOMAS MERTON

manage that involvement, however, is key. Do you see what I'm getting at here?

This understanding of *vocatio* became prominent during the Protestant Reformation through the work of Martin Luther. Up until that point, if you possessed a *vocatio* it meant that you were called to the church, which in turn meant that only priests and nuns really had a "calling" in life. But when Luther articulated the idea of the "priesthood of all believers," the notion of vocation was flattened. For Luther, the fact that every person was created in the image of God meant that every person was equally called to certain things in life—to the family, to God, to their community, to their occupation, to their nation. All of life is sacred and all of it can bring glory to God.

I could go on and on about this stuff, but I think you get the point. We don't just have one calling. All of us are actually "called" to various things that make life what it is. And this is one of the core assumptions for the flourishing life. I am reminded what Thomas Merton said, "Happiness is not a matter of intensity but of balance, order, rhythm and harmony." Chasing a realistic composite score across multiple callings is crucial to flourishing. Being a one-dimensional success story just can't nourish all we were meant to be. But at the same time, chasing a fantasy illusion of Super Joe will only kick us to the curb.

HOW TO FLOURISH IN YOUR WHOLE VOCATIO

Whenever I roll out this idea of multiple vocations, I consistently get the same questions: "Steve, I get that I have all these callings in life and that I need to learn how to manage them, but *how* do I do that?"

It's a fair question, and one that I think is best answered

with a few key principles. Over the years, I've found that these key ideas work not only for me, but also for many others that I've talked with. So, I want to offer you four ideas that I think are universally key in helping us flourish within our *vocatios*.

First, get over Super Joe and Tommy Bahama and call them what they are—a man-made marketing concoction. Make a visceral commitment to become whole, healthy, and complete, not perfect and superhuman.

Second, embrace the art of "the swap" to achieve balance. What I mean is this: After you let go of the idea of being "super" at everything, you must then acknowledge the related reality of life that sometimes you must swap time from one of your *vocatios* for another. Just like any tabletop has a limited capacity, so does my life. If your son or daughter has an important event coming up, then you may need to say "No" to a work function. That's pretty simple. But there are also certain seasons of work that demand more of your time, and that might steal a bit of time from your leisure or family time. That can be a harder pill to swallow.

Now here is my repositioning conviction that some might call heresy, but that I think is a necessary principle for a flourishing life. You should strive to score a solid B across the board in everything that matters over time. I have never met one man or woman who focuses on excelling in one area of life, while dismissing or failing in the others, who is truly flourishing. That type of compartmentalized, myopic living is fundamentally opposed to the flourishing life. Flourishing is really about chasing a realistic composite scorecard.

Third, create life rhythm. I love the good old-fashioned blue grass music of the south. In part, I love it because of the rhythm. You can't help but tap your foot and nod your head as you listen. Any kind of good music, though, is composed with a compelling rhythm. It ebbs and flows in crescendos and decrescendos. Some parts may rise to a roar, while others settle into a hush. That's the beauty of it. And that's the beauty of life as well. I try to establish a foundational rhythm and flow within and between all the areas of my life that matter most. This not only helps me manage each vocation appropriately, but it also helps manage expectations because everyone knows how things generally run.

What's your life rhythm? Do you have one? Or do you make it up as you go? I've found that when I allow work and family schedules and the tyranny of the immediate to dictate my schedule, I get stressed. To avoid this, I do my utmost to implement a Graves Rhythm and schedule life accordingly. Of course, the rhythm doesn't work magic every day. My life is still lived both from the outbox and the inbox in some kind of concert. But some proactively engineered rhythm can certainly help guide the dance moves.

Lastly, distinguish a "good idea" from a "divine mandate" and a "cultural expectation." In order to avoid falling off the rails in our *vocatios*, we must learn when to say "Yes," but also when to say "No" to people who pitch a "good idea" that seems compelling. Not every activity, pitch, and offer that comes your way is really a good, healthy helpful idea. At the same time, every good idea is NOT a divine mandate. It is up to me, and to you, to perceive the difference and know where to place my bits of time and energy. I must understand that whatever I say "Yes" to will ultimately steal time and energy away from my other callings in life. A swap is always going to happen when we say "Yes" to something.

In order to flourish, you must be discerning and be ready to say "No" to things that seem great at the moment but will ultimately knock you out of balance with your other, more important callings.

So often in this life we can feel like schizophrenic people— our heads whipping around because we're wheeling off to another work meeting, or we feel like we're failing our bodies and need to work out, or we haven't been to church in two months, or fill in the blank.

But we're not schizophrenic. That's simply the reality of life, but it's also its beauty. It demands much from us. It's multifaceted. It's intense. It's full of wonderful things to do, and wonderful people to know.

If you want to stop feeling like a schizophrenic person on the treadmill just take a breath and remember, you're not insane for feeling pulled in all directions. You are just neck deep in life. If you want peace, you must be okay with swapping time from one *vocatio* to another, establishing a life rhythm, and learning to discern what things you really need to be a part of. So, the next time you feel like your head is about snap off, just relax and breathe it all in. That's life.

HE HAS TOLD YOU, O MAN,
WHAT IS GOOD; AND WHAT
DOES THE LORD REQUIRE
OF YOU BUT TO DO JUSTICE,
TO LOVE KINDNESS, AND TO
WALK HUMBLY WITH YOUR
GOD? – MICAH 6:8 (ESV)

CHAPTER 5

BECOME A FARMER

The Importance of
Cultivating Deep Roots

"Deep roots are not reached by the frost."
– J.R.R. Tolkien

I HAVE A profound admiration of farmers. Their work, which uniquely joins in God's creative activity, requires a remarkable collection of skills and virtues. They are patient. They hold fast to an unparalleled work ethic, while simultaneously embracing a relaxed view of God's sovereignty—weather is the weather, the sun is the sun. They take great care in farming not only the plant we see, but also the root that supports it. They practice daily rhythms and cycles in their own lives and work, while also observing the rhythm and cycles of God's creation.

As the poet Wendell Berry puts it, farmers farm "for the love of farming." A farmer friend once told a story that beautifully captured this love. He was out driving his tractor in the alfalfa fields and came upon a lone, scared fawn. He stopped his tractor, hopped down, picked up the quivering creature, and returned to his tractor. And there he sat, holding the frightened and lost animal on his tractor, on a Maryland mountainside in an alfalfa field.

"I loved it," he said and then flashed a toothy grin. "It was just me and God and one of His beautiful little creatures."

I love the pure love and trust a farmer embodies. The agrarian life forces him to rely on the fruits of the land, nurtured and produced by elements he can't control. Does anyone take bigger risks on a daily basis? When Jesus told the parable of the talents, it was the worker who risked the most who then received the biggest reward.

The farmer is like one of his own plants—a blueberry bush perhaps. The roots of the bush rely solely on the rains and sunshine to fill them with enough strength and nourishment to bloom, to fill up with life and turn blue, rendering a delicious crop. The farmer realizes his roots—like those of the blueberry bush—must be nourished, cared for and cultivated, fertilized and fed.

What if we all operated with that level of trust and lived at peace with the inherent risk that comes from daily relying on something beyond ourselves? What if we could all endure the hardships of fierce winter storms and 4:00 a.m. wake ups during the farming season?

I wish I could be more like my farmer friend holding the fawn, spreading out my personal roots with each daily act of trust and commitment, of servitude and grace.

WHAT ARE ROOTS GOOD FOR?

Not all roots are created equal. Take, again, the blueberry bush. Its wiry roots don't go deep, but instead, they spread out then down. They're close to the surface and therefore cannot tap the water deposits in the deeper soil. They are dependent upon the constant care of watering or rains for their nourishment.

All roots, though, do perform the same basic tasks. They provide an entry point for the nourishment received from water and minerals. They provide the plant with stability, literally grounding the plant in a fixed position. The longer the plant lives and grows, the stronger the roots become entrenched in the soil.

Roots also provide the plant or tree with a certain degree of resiliency. Years ago, we experienced an intense ice storm, which among other things, damaged many of my beautiful maples. After the tree guy did some heavy pruning he told me, "They'll be ugly for a while, but they'll come back. You'll have to live with them being ugly for some time, but they'll be fine."

"THE ROOTS THAT PROVIDE
OUR RESILIENCY AND HELP
US STAND IN ADVERSITY
ARE NOT GROWN OVERNIGHT
OR IN SOME HIGH-TECH
ROOT INCUBATOR."

How will they come back? Why will they be fine? Simple—their roots. Even though their outer extremities were damaged, the core of their existence remained intact and even thrived.

We cannot neglect our roots. They possess the power to both sustain and save. Wise is the man who tends his roots.

Just like the roots of a plant, our roots, made up of things like faith and integrity, love and respect, will grow and become strong only when we remain vigilant to cultivate them. We must also remember one of the main elements of root growth: *time*. The roots that provide our resiliency and help us stand in adversity are not grown overnight or in some high-tech root incubator. They are strengthened over time, fed by the nutrients of experience, and cultivated by the wisdom of others.

As you consider your own root growth, ask yourself what your root system looks like. Is it like the blueberry bush that needs constant watering as the roots reach out across the surface of the soil? Or is it like the Pacific Willow tree with deep and unyielding roots?

OUR COMMUNITY, OUR ROOTS

There I was, sobbing like a little boy on a plane from Fayetteville to Chicago. It was a rough flight but I didn't notice it at the time. I was on my way to Nashville, via Chicago, and as is the case with most flights out of northwest Arkansas, I was on a small regional jet. If you've never had this unique pleasure, it means *extra* close seats and total strangers in your personal space.

Since I am still a paper-version book consumer, I always carry one of my four categories of books (fiction, business, theology, or biography) with me when traveling. On this particular trip I had brought along *The Little Way of Ruthie*

Leming and was well into the heart of it. I sat, reading a few pages and wiping my eyes, then reading a few more pages, and wiping my eyes—all the way to touch down. To provide a little context, I was already a bit emotionally unraveled, having just buried my college roommate and dear friend of 37 years only a month earlier. Heap on the fact that my wife and I were still adjusting and navigating empty-nestdom, and I may have been primed for a tear or two. Regardless, as the lines of Ruthie's story stacked one on top of the other, I broke into pieces.

I was a mess.

While I always love a deep-south tale, I wasn't ready for this surprise wrenching of my heart all framed around a simple, rural community in St. Francisville, Louisiana (pop. 1,700). Ruthie and her brother, Rod, grew up in this small town. Their community was deeply connected to its history—the kind that defines generations of families. It was the kind of community upheld by traditions, but even more so by one another. In the book, Rod tells the story of how he left St. Francisville in search of a career and a different life, and how Ruthie stayed and eventually contracted cancer.

The revelatory aspects of the book filter out through Ruthie's struggle with cancer, but even more so through how the community put their collective arms around her in a time of utmost need. This community love, in fact, was so strong for his sister that it prompted Rod to move his family back to St. Francisville so his own children could experience "the hidden grandeur and spiritual greatness" his sister experienced throughout her life in her small town.

After Ruthie passes, Rod reflects at her graveside. "Never would I have imagined," he begins, "that I would spend the morning of my little sister's forty-third birthday in the graveyard, watching workmen heave her tombstone into place. But nobody ever thinks about these things when they're young. Nobody thinks about limits, and how much we need each other. But if you live long enough, you see suffering. It comes close to you. It shatters the illusion, so dear to us, of self-sufficiency, of autonomy, of control. Look, a wife and mother, a good woman in the prime of her life, dying from cancer. It doesn't just happen to other people. It happens to your family. What do you do then?"[10]

What would *you* do? What would I do?

When we think of suffering and death, we sometimes miss the importance of family and community. But when we're in the mess of it all, when we find ourselves there, like Rod did, there is a huge need for special company that will come to your doorstep to help you carry on each day. The government won't do that and neither will insurance companies. "Only your family and community can do that."[11]

It's up to us to care for one another.

THE PICTURE OF ROOTS

The story of Ruthie is a grand picture of someone with roots. And none were stronger than community. Community necessarily has a geographic element to it. It is a place. Roots need locale. We may think social media and virtual communications can substitute for real neighbors, but Ruthie didn't buy it. Community, *real community*—the kind where you can touch and even smell another person, is built on deep relationships. It has texture and that certain something that can't be "webbed" on the World Wide Web.

When life hits the wall, spins out on the curve, overwhelms us, confounds even the sharpest of us, totally beats us down, or just simply disappoints us, this is when our roots are tested. Or when we happen upon magnificent success we find a

"WHEN LIFE HITS THE WALL, SPINS OUT ON THE CURVE, OVERWHELMS US, CONFOUNDS EVEN THE SHARPEST OF US, TOTALLY BEATS US DOWN, OR JUST SIMPLY DISAPPOINTS US, THIS IS WHEN OUR ROOTS ARE TESTED."

testing of a different weather pattern. Those of us who spend the time to cultivate deep roots will find that thriving doesn't equal good times or bad times. Thriving equals endurance.

We all have a sub-surface structure that exists as the foundation of our life, a root system within. Those interior roots—made of belief, conviction, and truth—can really only do so much. They must be supported and nourished, even healed, by something from without.

Thankfully, we also possess an exterior roots system, the kind made up of the people and places around us. In a world where suffering not only exists but is a constant presence, pounding on us each day, it's no secret that our community of family and friends carries much weight.

I love how Eugene Peterson captures this truth in his own paraphrase of a famous verse in Ecclesiastes. *"By yourself you're unprotected. With a friend you can face the worst. Can you round up a third? A three-stranded rope isn't easily snapped"* (4:12 MSG). This is put so well, its truth is self-evident. We're better together.

I may be a mystic hillbilly fisherman, but I don't live on an island or in a mountain cave. I'm not so naïve, or so old, that I don't realize the importance and even the need for the digital applications that enhance our communications. Technology enables us to communicate in ways our forefathers never dreamed. But I will never substitute the real for the virtual. I try not to give precedence to my phone when a real person is standing in front of me. We've become distracted by our gadgets and often miss out on the *real* moments of life. As you read this page, you're living in the now. When you set this book down and discuss it with your friend, you're living in the now. But more and more it seems like folks would rather be somewhere else—not in the now, but in the land of Over There.

If we're not careful, we'll jeopardize the intimacy of relationships because of distraction. Nothing great happens in this world through unhealthy distraction. Singular focus, on the other hand, does produce greatness. The singular focus of enjoying dinner with friends—no devices, no notifications—produces deep friendships and memories. The singular focus of worshipping at your church with the family of God produces spiritual intimacy within your congregation. The singular focus of throwing the football with your son or dressing up like a clown with your daughter produces trust and a relational bond not easily broken. The singular focus of working on a project with a colleague can produce a cultural good, a deep friendship and innovation. When we're not distracted, we're present. And when we're present, we water others. We deepen ourselves. We thrive.

ROOT HARMONY

It took tragedy to remind Rod of the importance of community—of establishing deep roots in an actual place where the collisions of people mark and enhance life on a daily basis. I pray that you and I will see and embrace the wisdom that Rod now understands firsthand. That having a support group, being connected to family and friends, and simplifying our lives are some of life's most precious keys. And we should guard those keys with everything we've got.

Even though we're not all farmers and we don't live in a constant state of risk, perhaps we should all aspire to emulate the farmer. Perhaps we should strive to trust like the farmer, to understand the importance of personal nourishment, and to care and cultivate our roots.

Ruthie was fortunate to live in a veritable greenhouse of farmers—all living and nourishing one another. That is what Rod witnessed as his sister slipped away. Without each other, without our shared spaces, we're nothing but unprotected and isolated creatures fumbling for an existence that we can't find, because it was meant to be lived in the harmony of deep-rooted community.

"A FARMER PLANTED SEED. AS HE
SCATTERED THE SEED, SOME OF IT
FELL ON THE ROAD AND BIRDS ATE
IT. SOME FELL IN THE GRAVEL; IT
SPROUTED QUICKLY BUT DIDN'T
PUT DOWN ROOTS, SO WHEN THE
SUN CAME UP IT WITHERED JUST
AS QUICKLY. SOME FELL IN THE
WEEDS; AS IT CAME UP, IT WAS
STRANGLED AMONG THE WEEDS AND
NOTHING CAME OF IT. SOME FELL ON
GOOD EARTH AND CAME UP WITH A
FLOURISH, PRODUCING A HARVEST
EXCEEDING HIS WILDEST DREAMS."

–MARK 4:4-8 (MSG)

CHAPTER 6

GO FOR THE LONG TAIL

*Perspective Changes
Everything*

"Try not to become a man of success but a man of value."
– Albert Einstein

IN 2008 CHRIS Anderson, editor for *Wired* magazine, wrote a provocative book called *The Long Tail: Why the Future of Business Is Selling Less of More*. It quickly became a *New York Times* best seller and has become a standard read for folks in media and publishing. In the book, Anderson challenges producers to think more significantly about products in terms of their longevity, rather than simply trying to make a quick splash that is eventually swept away in a tidal wave of other newer products. As he builds this thesis, Anderson provides a brilliant cultural analysis of buying and selling trends. He explains that consumers once faced limited alternatives. A few places to buy movies, books, and music. A few major outlets. One, maybe two versions, of a concept. Today, however, our options are practically endless, and this is especially true when it comes to media. With little effort, almost anyone anywhere can search myriad alternatives to purchase or stream content. For Anderson, this means that in order to survive in the current media market, producers must adopt a long view for their products. They must understand how a product will perform over time. Is it a product that was made with the "past" in mind? Did its creators consider how they might create something that isn't just trendy, but that contains a timeless quality?

While you and I may not be gearing up for a product launch or a movie release, we are, every minute of every day, engaged in the launching of our lives. We are constantly moving into the future, eating up the present, waving good-bye to the past. The speed at which our society operates has become the perfect incubator for the obsolescence of things. So perfect, in fact, that planned obsolescence of products is now a consumer reality. But these cultural tendencies don't just affect things, they affect people too.

It's easy to live with a now-or-never attitude toward life, adopting the same short-sighted attitude we find in our throwaway culture. Speed and immediacy, though, simply do not contribute positively to a flourishing life. We flourish not when we run breathlessly from task to task, but rather when we find ourselves at rest *within* time. What I mean by *within* time is simply that in order to flourish we must maintain a proper view of what lies before us as well as considering the affect our lives have on what collects behind us. This is what a "long view" of life does for us. It helps us get beyond the immediate to both see down the road clearly, and to face the past with little regret.

Think about it for a moment. How do you measure your life? If your answer has something, or everything, to do with the immediate, then you likely need to broaden your horizon and consider a longer view of life. When we measure success with a transactional mindset, only cognizant of present consequences, we cheapen our legacy. We fail to realize how dramatically our shortsightedness affects our understanding of success and failure. You and I don't really know if something fails or succeeds until after the fact; meaning, we must wait and see. Waiting demands a long view of life, patience *within* time to see what happens. When we live with a long view we are, in effect, considering what and how our life decisions will affect our futures and also our pasts. When, on the other hand, we make a decision based only on the here-and-now, we're left with a here-and-now legacy, a here-and-now future—which is really no future at all.

"A LONG VIEW HELPS US
REACT WITH TEMPERANCE
AND CALMNESS NOT ONLY
TO FAILURE, BUT ALSO
TO SUCCESS."

I recently led a conversation about kingdom movements to a group of high-energy Christian young entrepreneurs. During the prep time I found myself re-reading about William Wilberforce, Martin Luther, and St. Ignatius Loyola, among others. All of these leaders were sterling examples of heroic leadership and undoubtedly had a long view of life and impact. Just Google each of these leaders sometime and be inspired by their "long tail."

A long view helps us react with temperance and calmness not only to failure, but also to success. We're not destroyed when something doesn't pan out with our new entrepreneurial venture. We're not flattened when a certain stock crashes, or when we do poorly on a test in college. Why? Because we're resting *within* time, realizing that what happens right here, right now does not define and does not doom our futures. Likewise, a long view allows us to drink in success with humility, realizing that our temporal gains, though sweet and worthy of celebration, are merely a drop in the bucket of life.

This reminds me of something called *The Echo Effect*. Essentially it is the reverberation of our choices back to us. Some decisions take longer than others to bounce back and some decisions bounce back harder than others. Over time we find ourselves in a full reverberation in our life as a whole. When we reach our older life, our early life begins to bounce back to us. Everything we do echoes in this life. We just don't always realize it on the front side.

So, a long view of life helps me contextualize my behavior; as well as contextualize what's happening to me. Think about a professional athlete who sprains her ankle. In order to avoid further aggravation of the same injury and to ensure the longevity of her career, she must lay off her ankle for a significant period of time. She must take a long view of her career. If she begins working out the very next day, or simply numbs the pain with an injection, she will run the risk of ruining her ankle for further play. And the echo of that decision will be disappointing.

MORE THAN AN ECHO

While it is helpful to think about the echo effect that our perspectives play upon our lives, it is also enjoyable to consider the energizing characteristics that accompany a long view of life, a living *within* time.

Such a view helps develop unfortunately rare character traits like hope, patience, and endurance. In his letter to the church in Rome, the Apostle Paul points to these exact traits, as he reminds us to *"Rejoice in hope, be patient in tribulation, be constant in prayer" (Romans 12:12 ESV)*. In spite of some incredible circumstances in his own life, Paul was able to advocate the long view of life because he believed unswervingly in God's sovereignty. Difficult life circumstances often make it challenging for us to wade through tribulation with Paul's attitude, rejoicing in something we may not see. When, however, you and I live in anticipation and expectation for what the future holds, we are much more likely to cling to the hope Paul describes—the hope of a way out, an answer to our problem, a provision for our need.

When we understand that life doesn't end when something bad happens, we also realize that we can keep hope in focus as life stretches out in front of us and that we can make it through the shadows—we can *flourish*. This idea always brings to mind a favorite quote from the gutsy Brit himself, Winston Churchill: "Success is not final, failure is not fatal: it is the courage to continue that counts." Those are the words of a man who saw life stretch out before him—vast and dewy with opportunity. If a man like Churchill, who frankly faced greater challenges than most of us will ever encounter, can live with such a perspective, then we too should be inspired to see past everyday troubles and realize that we flourish when we overcome.

A long view of life isn't just about persevering through struggles; it also helps us relax. When everything isn't tied up in the present and in immediate reactions, we become more accepting. Small slights and inconveniences carry less weight, and forgiveness comes more easily. We come to care more about the health of lasting relationships and less about the immediate hurt of a callous comment. This is critical for the flourishing life. If I collect a bunch of broken relationships because I can't see past my most recent hurt or disappointment, then I'll likely end up a bitter old man who would rather wither in my own shortsightedness than flourish in my long view of life.

"But wait a minute, Steve. Is it wrong, then, to live in the moment—to enjoy it and savor it?"

That's a fair question.

I'm not trying to radically divorce us from the present and keep us from enjoying the here-and-now. Theologians have for years embraced a "now and not yet" mindset. It is the idea that the true spiritual reality has a *now* element and a *not yet*—a future element. What I am doing is encouraging us to maintain a perspective that doesn't simply look down at our feet, but also keeps an eye on the road ahead. That doesn't mean we neglect what is in front of us. On the contrary! I think we embrace and enjoy the present in an even more meaningful way when we possess a long view of life. This is because a long view gives us peace for the moment, hope for

"OVER TIME WE FIND
OURSELVES IN A FULL
REVERBERATION IN OUR
LIFE AS A WHOLE."

the future, and an attitude of "I'll learn from my mistakes" regarding the past.

I have several friends that ride mountain bikes. One of them recently explained to me the importance of "looking through the turn" when riding. What he meant is that when you're approaching a tight turn you should keep one eye on the ground in front of you, so that you don't veer off the path, but also look through the turn and down the path. This allows a rider to prepare for what lies ahead and see what is coming up. It doesn't mean they're not "in it" at that moment. It doesn't mean they're not enjoying the winding trail. It means that by keeping their vision down the path, they are actually able to better enjoy the part of the path they're on. I love that—and that's what I'm saying here.

The flourishing life is the flowering life—and that happens right now, in a moment, and also continues into the next moment, and the next. I'd be an ignorant farmer if I decided not to enjoy the apples growing on my apple trees. But I'd be equally foolish if I decided to eat them all right now and not plan for the winter.

A THOUGHT ON LEGACY

At the end of every season my son's basketball coach used to deliver a simple message: "Do not let high school basketball be the best thing or worst thing that has ever happened to you in your life. If it is, then we've failed as coaches." What did he mean? He was communicating to those young players the importance of a long view of life. He was telling them, you have a long life and basketball should fit appropriately in that life, but it does not define your life. In short, it's not your legacy. Sure, one phenom might be the next Kevin Durant, but most kids with a high school letter jacket won't play pro ball or even college ball. Most will enjoy basketball for a time and then spend their life doing something completely unrelated to a round ball going through a net.

Let me wrap up this chapter by considering the lives and wisdom of two Abrahams. In the book of Hebrews the writer tells us about Abraham's great faith, and it's worth our reflection. *"By faith Abraham, when called to go to a place he would later receive as his inheritance, obeyed and went, even though he did not know where he was going. By faith he made his home in the promised land like a stranger in a foreign country; he lived in tents, as did Isaac and Jacob, who were heirs with him of the same promise. For he was looking forward to the city with foundations, whose architect and builder is God"* (Hebrews 11:8-10 NIV). Now there is a guy with a long-term view of meaning, value, and significance.

Abraham was able to live a transient kind of life for many years because he trusted God with his future, and because he believed in an ultimate vision and goal for his life—eternal life with the Creator God. This foundation incited his forward-looking perspective and emboldened his faith. It's amazing what we can accomplish, what we're willing to wade through, and how far we're willing to travel when our hearts are firmly secured in the hand of God. To pull in Churchill yet again, he said, "The farther back you can look, the farther forward you are likely to see." I think the former Prime Minister is talking about looking back over the tough times that you've been through and realizing that you're still walking—you're still living, you're still keeping-on-keeping-on. Maybe he wasn't referencing the reality of a God who carries us through all those times, but I like to think about it in those terms.

Carl Sandburg talking about the impact of the other renowned Abraham (Lincoln) said, "A tree is best measured *after* it was fallen."[12] That is when we are able to capture the breadth and length and width of its girth. The rings of life experience speak volumes to our friends and family. They give us proof of a flourishing tree or one that was suffering through rot and disease. A flourishing tree impacts generations; the rotting tree barely survives its own.

Which are you?

> May the righteous flourish in his days and
> prosperity abound until the moon is no more.
> – Psalm 72:7 (HCSB)

THERE IS HOPE FOR A TREE:
IF IT IS CUT DOWN, IT WILL
SPROUT AGAIN, AND ITS
SHOOTS WILL NOT DIE. IF
ITS ROOTS GROW OLD IN
THE GROUND AND ITS STUMP
STARTS TO DIE IN THE SOIL,
THE SMELL OF WATER MAKES
IT THRIVE AND PRODUCE
TWIGS LIKE A SAPLING.
– JOB 14:7-9 (HCSB)

CHAPTER 7

YOUR MOVING CENTER

*How Love
Covers All*

"Love takes up where knowledge leaves off."
– Thomas Aquinas

CONTEMPORARY CHRISTIAN CULTURE loves love. While previous generations primarily conceived and spoke of God in terms of His power, or justice, or even wrath, we love that "God is love." Our language, whether from the pulpit or across the dinner table is saturated with "love language." Unsurprisingly, then, we've also become quite fond of reading and writing on the topic, as is evidenced by the recent popularity of books about love. In one of these titles, *Love Does*, Bob Goff explains how love incites us to "do." In another, more controversial book, *Love Wins*, Rob Bell challenges readers with the quality and range of God's love—how far and wide it covers us, how it affects our ethics, how we in turn show it to the world. Both books hit the *New York Times* Best Seller List. It appears just about everyone wants to understand love.

What I find fascinating about these two books is their focus on love's movement. Most of us realize that saying "I love you" to someone carries a much greater weight if that person also sees our actions prove those words to be true. But what must not be missed is that in order for you and I to express true and loving action, love must first exist within and move out from a heart that is true.

In their book, *Veneer: Living Deeply in a Surface Society*, my friends Timothy Willard and Jason Locy describe love as an aspect of "The Language of God." They show how the "Language of Culture," which consists of technological progress, consumption, and celebrity culture, often operates in direct contradiction to love in that it encourages individuals to live for themselves.

The Language of Culture says, "Use technology to build your own platform, because in a world where celebrity fame equals cultural currency you need to get all you can." So, we mirror a culture that emphasizes self-promotion, greed, and material success as the epitome of self-development. The culture says if you love yourself the right way then you'll want these "things," and it points to things that satisfy an individual.

For the Christian, however, a love that moves is a love that simmers in our souls first. It's a love that exists as a result of our Creator's love for us. Because of His love for us, we, in turn, yearn with affection for Him *and* move in love and good deeds for one another. "We love because He first loved us."

Without that anchoring concept of love, our energy for people and things can get confusing. A pastor friend of mine likes to say:

Problems don't arise because we need things, or because we love things, or because of the things themselves that we love and need. Problems arise when we fail to grasp the nature of the objects that we need and love, the manner in which we love them, and the expectations we have regarding the outcome of our love.

Because of these actual differences in things, the outcome of loving each actual thing will be different. There is a divinely designed fit between our needs, the character of the things that can satisfy them, and the way we should love them in order to be satisfied. Even though each thing God made is good, delightful, legitimate, and a source of satisfaction as an object of our love, we must not expect more from it than its unique nature can provide. We must give love and praise to things apportioned to their worth.

According to Augustine, "There is a scale of value stretching from earthly to heavenly realities, from the visible to the invisible; and the inequality between these goods make possible the existence of them all." God is one thing, angels are another; as are people, red oaks, squash, rocks, and dirt, each item fits in God's overall scheme of creation. The nature of things in hierarchy is unchangeable and so is the kind of satisfaction it can provide when we are related to it through love.

The love God has for us and the return love we have for Him stands in a unique relationship. It should have no equal. We were created with a desire to be loved. But that is not all.

I WANT TO BE KNOWN

We want to be known. By God. By ourselves. By others.

We don't *just* want to be known, though. We want to be known AND loved. We want someone to look at us, see who we really are, and not only accept what they see, but to find it pleasing. When we feel this, this twin emotion of vulnerability and embrace, we somehow feel greater than ourselves. We feel a sense of connectedness, of mutual knowledge.

This is the emotion we feel when our child or spouse expresses their love. When the people that know us best, that have seen our worst, love us well it's like a surge of adrenaline. It gives us an unbelievable confidence—that someone who knows us so intimately could still love us so profoundly. What an enormous shot in the arm, to be known by someone else, to feel their love, and to live in that reality!

This is what we all desire—to be known, to be loved.

And yet, at the very same time, we also want to revel in our uniqueness—that very thing that we desire others to cherish with unconditional affection. We want to somehow rise above the apparent sameness of the world and be ourselves. So, even though we crave to be known and loved by others, we also thirst for a kind of self-love, that kind of love that sees and celebrates ourselves as unique.

This, however, is where things get dangerous. The forces and influences of the world say, "Be yourself!" And so we do just that…and we glory in it. Therein lies the problem—not in the "being" but in the "glorying."

When we begin to glory in our uniqueness, we unconsciously begin to neglect the outward direction of love's movement. We drift from the underlying principle that propels those who know us and love us well—the unconditional nature of their love. We begin to love "because" of things. As odd as it may sound, we even begin to love ourselves because of what we have to offer.

When I start believing my own bio or admiring my own resume, I begin to drift into a place that is all Steve. Work becomes a great place for *me* to flex my entrepreneurial muscle. Family becomes a place for *me* to dominate and be the center of attention. My community becomes a theater for the Steve Show—what can I do to show others how great I am.

Regardless of how noble my intentions may be, when I start working from a place of, "Hey, look at Steve," I've lost the reins on my motives.

In his autobiography, *Surprised by Joy*, C.S. Lewis tells the story of his early life and his conversion to Christianity. The narrative, which he frames as a pilgrimage, explores the ongoing tension we are discussing, the tension between a love of self and a love that moves. For Lewis the journey to Christianity wasn't a simple, or quick, one. Rather than simply diving into his faith as a young man, he grapples with it for years, before slowly moving to a place of total devotion. A

"WHEN I REALLY
LOVE SOMEONE ELSE
IT MAKES THEIR
NARRATIVE AS
IMPORTANT TO ME
AS MY OWN."

major part of Lewis's journey involved his previous belief in an "Absolute." This absolute was essentially a concept; there was no person at all, let alone Jesus Christ, attached to it. "This quasi-religion," writes Lewis, "was all a one-way street, all *eros* steaming up, but no *agape* darting down. There was nothing to fear; better still, nothing to obey."[13]

We often say we desire an *agape* love, the kind of love that darts down, as Lewis puts it; a kind of love that is defined by the action of sacrifice. In reality, though, we are usually far too comfortable with an *eros* kind of love; a love that steams up and makes us feel good about ourselves, a love that focuses on *us* and our feelings and our well-being.

A cozy, feel-good kind of love, however, is neither sustainable nor fulfilling. Life simply does not expand into a constant crescendo of ooey-gooey *eros*. On the contrary, it dips and rises like the beat of a heart. We need a love that is able to sustain us through these highs and lows, not a love that ignores reality and simply gives us a shot in the arm.

WHAT LOVE DOES

The flourishing life is a life marked by love-giving. In what follows, I want to take some time to provide you with some powerful revelations that I've been fortunate enough to encounter regarding the action of love.

Love Muscles Us Off the Center Stage

When I really love someone else it makes their narrative as important to me as my own. Christ said, love others as you love yourself. When I begin to love other people I begin to find myself out of the spotlight. I find myself promoting the work of others. I find myself giving energy to the projects of others. I find myself seeking the success of my colleagues and clients.

Putting others ahead of ourselves is revolutionary. Pulitzer Prize writer Jeffrey Marx captured the story of what he calls the most remarkable sports team he has ever seen; a group of high school football players coached to love deeply. In *Season of Life*, Marx retells his time with Joe Ehrmann, the highly awarded pro bowl player who, after retirement, directed his energy into coaching the young players at Gilmore High. He built a championship team around love. "The coaches would gather the eighty boys together and shout out, 'What is our job?' Biff asked on behalf of himself, Joe, and the eight other assistant coaches. 'To love us,' most of the boys yelled back. The older boys had already been through this routine more than enough times to know the proper answer. The younger boys, new to Gilmore football, would soon catch on.

"'And what is *your* job?' Biff shot back. 'To love each other,' the boys responded. Marx said he came to realize that this standard exchange was just as much a part of Gilmore football as running or tackling. 'I don't care if you're big or small, huge muscles or no muscles, never even played football or the star on the team—I don't care about any of that stuff,' the coaches told the young players. 'If you are here, then you are one of us, and we love you. Simple as that.'" [14]

You have to admit, promoting the other person and love is not the norm that most successful sports teams are built upon. But pure love, when it is released, is catalytic in the hearts of those in its path. And with a long view, love can become a shaper of more real success than perhaps any other instrument.

Love Sanitizes Our Motives

I touched on this earlier, but it's worth repeating—our motives are shifty emotions. We, in fact, don't even completely

"IF I LOVE ALL PEOPLE,
THEN I WILL HAVE TO
LOVE PEOPLE WHO AREN'T
LOVABLE, WHO AREN'T
LOVELY, AND WHO DON'T
RECIPROCATE MY LOVE."

understand our own motives. As King Solomon warned, "We justify our actions by appearances; God examines our motives." It's easy to look at an outcome that *appears* positive and justify the reasons we're doing this or that. But God knows our motives. If we're not motivated by God's love, then our intentions are necessarily less than what they could be.

If, on the other hand, we operate out of pure love, our motives become clean; they are purified. This truth is foundational to the Christian faith. If you and I follow hard after Christ, then something amazing occurs: We begin to look like Him. I don't mean we start to physically look like God. I mean our hearts attach to His heart. Our moral vision for life comes from His moral goodness. His ambition for us becomes our ambition for ourselves—to love and serve our fellow man.

My motives find themselves wrapped up in a big God-blanket that covers me completely. And when I'm wrapped in that, my life not only finds purpose, but also the security I find in being *known* by Him.

Love Pushes Me into a Deeper Dependence on Jesus

If I am serious about making God's love the core of my being, then my life should and will look very different—it should stick out in a world of self-love sameness. God's love demands that I walk the plank daily for my friends and family, dying to myself and serving others. God's love demands that I give up the motives tirelessly driving me toward fame and success because if I love God, then I will trust *Him* with whatever accomplishment or notoriety He might bring. If I love God, then I will place my heart in His hands with regard to my relationships, even though it may feel unsafe at times.

But it doesn't stop with just my family and friends.

God commands us to love our neighbor as ourselves…
and His definition of *neighbor* extends much further than
our comfortable cul-de-sac. If I love all people, then I will
have to love people who aren't lovable, who aren't lovely, and
who don't reciprocate my love. This, though, is actually the
love I was made for—a God love. The late writer Brennan
Manning had this type of love in mind when he encouraged
an audience to love more deeply—"Instead of being identified
as a community that memorizes Scripture," said Manning,
"why not be identified as a community of professional lovers
that cause people to say 'How they love one another!' … When
you interact with someone, you are going to leave them feeling
a little better or a little worse. You may affirm them, or you
may deprive them, but there'll be no neutral exchange. If we
as a Christian community took seriously the idea that the
representation of our love for Jesus is our love for one another,
I am convinced it would change the world."[15]

However, if we're not depending on God, then we're
probably not loving Him like we should. And if we're not
loving Him as we should, it's unlikely that we're loving one
another as we should, let alone the world. The flourishing life
is a life totally dependent on God—cast at His feet in service
to others.

Love Is Transformational

Throughout this chapter, I have hinted that true love is
active love. While this is certainly true, let me clarify just a
bit. It is popular to say that "Love does" and that "Love wins,"
but love is not just a wild blur of activity. It begins within
our hearts. It begins as our soul responds to God's love with
affection and surrender and worship. Our God is a jealous
God, and He wants us first for Himself. He wants our

faithfulness and our love for Him. Our actions follow these affections. What begins in the heart finds expression in the kindness of human action.

It's amazing just how many action-based assumptions accompany *agape* love in the Scriptures. In Paul's famous love chapter alone—1 Corinthians 13—they are seemingly everywhere. We must remember, though, that the action does not come first. The action follows a heart filled with God's love. He pours His love into us. He grants us graces, He gifts us with mercy, He anoints us with blessings, and from that overflow we love—in word and in deed. *This* is what love does, and this is what a life needs to flourish. Without such a love, we wither.

Consider the journey of a little seed to help frame the transformational power of a giving love. The seed must go down into the earth and experience a kind of dying. There it lies in the cold earth, but in its dying, in its "going down," something miraculous happens. It splits open and sprouts life. It's not just any life, but a life that also gives life. As the sprout of life breaks through the topsoil it reaches for the sun in a tender climb of new birth. It weathers the heavy rains of spring, the heat of summer, the winds of autumn, and the cold of winter. The seed, once buried deep in the earth, now climbs into the air, giving beauty, giving air, giving fruit, giving and giving. It flourishes, even though the seasons come and go. It flourishes as it grows, spreading its roots into the same place that once acted as its tomb. It moves and reaches up, spreading out and digging deep. The flourishing life is a life of movement, a life of love that digs and reaches, a life that climbs and spreads for the sake of others. It is a giving life.

Without a love that rises from within, and then turns itself outward, we cannot flourish. We will not flourish.

If I speak with human eloquence and angelic ecstasy but don't love, I'm nothing but the creaking of a rusty gate. If I speak God's Word with power, revealing all his mysteries and making everything plain as day, and if I have faith that says to a mountain, "Jump," and it jumps, but I don't love, I'm nothing. If I give everything I own to the poor and even go to the stake to be burned as a martyr, but I don't love, I've gotten nowhere. So, no matter what I say, what I believe, and what I do, I'm bankrupt without love.

Love never gives up.
Love cares more for others than for self.
Love doesn't want what it doesn't have.
Love doesn't strut,
Doesn't have a swelled head,
Doesn't force itself on others, Isn't always "me first,"
Doesn't fly off the handle,
Doesn't keep score of the sins of others,
Doesn't revel when others grovel,
Takes pleasure in the flowering of truth,
Puts up with anything,
Trusts God always,
Always looks for the best,
Never looks back,
But keeps going to the end.
– 1 Corinthians 13:1-7 (MSG)

THERE IS NO FEAR IN LOVE;
BUT PERFECT LOVE CASTS
OUT FEAR, BECAUSE FEAR
INVOLVES PUNISHMENT,
AND THE ONE WHO FEARS IS
NOT PERFECTED IN LOVE.
WE LOVE, BECAUSE HE
FIRST LOVED US.
–1 JOHN 4:18-19 (NASB)

CHAPTER 8

GO DEEP, GIVE MUCH

*The Secret Is Investing in
Things That Matter*

"No one has ever become poor by giving."
– Anne Frank

WHO DO YOU want to see flourish? What cause or mission has a gravitational pull for you?

It sounds like a simple question. At first glance, it may even seem rather vague and unimportant. After all, if you and I were honest, more often than not our answer would be "nobody." We would say, "I'm too busy to have energy for anyone but me." That might sound harsh, but it's probably true.

Changing how I answered that question has improved my life in profound ways.

Early on in my life, most of what I did was for me. To get one step ahead. To go one mile further. To climb one more rung on the ladder of success. Things changed for me, though, when I truly began to understand the value of people.

We live in a leverage-happy society. Relationships aren't just relationships, they're platforms for leverage and tools for networking. Even networking itself has lost much of its relational quality. When all we want to do is hopscotch from one relationship to the next, the relationships themselves tend to matter very little. The problem here is self-evident. People should not be leveraged. People are not objects to be "used." People are not stepping-stones to our next success story.

People matter. They shape our lives. They shape our world. They are our culture. When we start dehumanizing people, using them as disposable game pieces in our great connect-the-dots career game, we diminish not only the individuals, but our culture as well.

Listen to David Brooks on this matter. "I've come to think

"SACRIFICIALLY
HELPING OTHERS IS
A RARE THING. IN
FACT, I THINK IT'S
ALMOST BEEN LOST
IN OUR CULTURE."

that flourishing consists of putting yourself in situations in which you lose self-consciousness and become fused with other people, experiences, or tasks. It happens sometimes when you are lost in a hard challenge, or when an artist or craftsman becomes one with the brush or the tool. It happens sometimes while you're playing sports or listening to music or lost in a story, or to some people when the feel enveloped by God's love. And it happens most when we connect with other people. I've come to think that happiness isn't really produced by conscious accomplishments. Happiness is a measure of how thickly the unconscious parts of our minds are intertwined with other people and with activities. Happiness is determined by how much information and affection flows through us covertly every day and year."

GIVE, TAKE, TRADE

In recent years, I've asked several very successful friends this question: "How important are your relationships with people to the flourishing of your personal life and the success of your business?" They always respond with one word: *vital.* Not surprisingly, then, the folks I know who are the most successful in life are also very rich in relationships. These men and women invest not only their time, but they invest their energy into the projects of other people. They invest their resources in order to help others succeed, and they put their money where their relationships are by investing hard-earned dollars into others. Is this true of you and your relationships?

Where do you invest your energy?

Where do you invest your experience and skills?

Where do you invest your money?

The answers to these questions help me determine how deeply I'm investing in my relationships. In short, they reveal my relational heart. Do I have the heart of a Giver, a Taker, or a Trader?

We all know what a relational Taker is. No one wants to be one, and no one wants to work with one. Takers aren't flourishers. Instead, a Taker is always keeping accounts. He is always asking, "What do people owe me?" or "How can I get a leg up?"

A Trader, on the other hand, is a person who is always trading one thing for another—always bartering, always giving, but also always taking. A Trader is sly; they do things in business and in relationships for the sake of the transactions, in order to make a trade. They always hold a little something back, so that in the future they can use it, by trading it for a little bit of that.

When I was a young man my mother helped me learn how to not keep score with people. It is insulting to be with relational takers—the ones who live with a running ledger that defines and throttles the level of depth and authenticity of their relationships. And it is exhausting to be with relational traders—the ones who live by "If I'm doing this thing for you, you can do that for me," muddying the waters of their relationships.

Givers, however, always trump Takers and Traders in the flourishing hierarchy. They give freely, and they give often. They give their time, their talents, and their resources, and when they do this, their flourishing bank account gets big. In contrast, our flourishing bank account suffers when we're focused on calling accounts due and bent on trading this for that.

When you find a Giver, you find someone who wants to pour into the agendas and passions of others. You find someone who has energy for other people, not just when or if it benefits them, but because they care about the person and desire to help them.

Become a relational Giver!

THE MAGICAL POWER OF GOODNESS

The act of sacrificially helping others unlocks a profound power of goodness within ourselves and within those around us. We are drawn to it and compelled to advance it. This draw exists, I would suggest, because we all carry some measure of God's goodness within our souls. It's imprinted upon us at birth—it's part of the *imago Dei* (image of God). In the same vein, we have an equally strong but opposite reaction to evil. Think about how you react toward villains in a book or movie. There is an almost visceral response because there is something within those individuals that we want eradicated, destroyed, or fixed.

Goodness, though, draws us toward resolution and reconciliation. It draws us toward the truth of a situation and the truth about others. The power of goodness manifests itself as one gives up his or her own right or privilege in service of another. When you encounter such a person or observe such an action, you unmistakably see how profound the power of goodness is.

Think about the Good Samaritan story. When we read it, we smile—goodness alights on our soul. Sacrificially helping others is a rare thing. In fact, I think it's almost been lost in our culture.

"But Steve," you say, "philanthropy has never been stronger. More than ever people are giving and helping others."

I would not argue with you about the current rise of philanthropy and the growing charity work all over the globe. I agree that more than ever, people care. What I'm trying to do is get beyond the "caring" and dig down to the quality of that "caring." The Good Samaritan story moves us not just because the Samaritan cares. No, we are affected by the story because of the lengths to which the Samaritan goes to secure the safety and well-being of a complete stranger.

The Samaritan's goodness began with awareness. He noticed an injured and bleeding man on the side of the road. To that point, though, his story was no different than the others who saw the injured man and kept on walking. After awareness, however, we see his care manifest in the action of stopping, helping that man up, and carrying him to safety. But he doesn't just drop him off and leave. The Samaritan attends his wounds, he provides him with nourishment, and he financially supports the injured man's recovery.

In all of this we tend to forget about the Samaritan's day. Where was he going? What did he have on his calendar for that day? Was he on his way to an important meeting? Was he headed to check in on his investments, his vineyard, or other properties? Was he taking a "holiday" or vacation day to visit old friends in another town? We don't know, but we do know that wherever he was going and whatever he was doing, he sacrificed the one commodity we all seem to be short of: *time!*

The Samaritan made real sacrifices for a person he didn't even know. This gives us a glimpse into his worldview—how he cared for his fellow man, how he viewed relationships and the value of others. His hierarchy of values had human beings at the top, deserving of our deepest and most valuable sacrifices.

Think again for a moment about that growing pool of philanthropists. It's fantastic that they give, and that they give so much. But what if they *really* gave—until it hurt, until they could feel the pinch of sacrifice as C.S. Lewis suggests?

"I do not believe one can settle how much we ought to give. I am afraid the only safe rule is to give more than we can spare. In other words, if our expenditure on comforts, luxuries, amusements, etc., is up to the standard common among those with the same income as our own, we are probably giving away too little. If our charities do not at all pinch or hamper us, I should say they are too small. There ought to be things we should like to do and cannot do because our charitable expenditure excludes them." [16]

And what about you and me? What if our giving, what if our pouring into others wasn't just a duty but a way of life? What if sacrifice was the language we spoke to everyone, and they not only heard it, but also knew and felt it? The world would change overnight!

When someone gives sacrificially, a profound power of goodness is unleashed. The Good Samaritan wasn't a full-time caregiver to people. He wasn't a Red Cross volunteer or a new not-for-profit to the homeless and broken. He had something to do, he had an agenda, he was busy. He was on his way somewhere for some reason, *but* when he came upon a need, he gave of his time and his energy and his money. He interrupted his routine, took a risk, gave deeply, and helped someone else.

WHEN OTHERS FLOURISH, YOU FLOURISH

Most people are familiar with the financial model that possesses residual returns—constant dividends are paid on something that never touches the principal. In the same way, people who give sacrificially gain perpetual returns. Their investment into the lives of others continues to grow as those people grow and mature in their projects, families, and vocations.

Think about people who've invested well. Even during difficult times, they continue to flourish financially. Why? Unless it is pure luck, their portfolio reflects some diversity, some depth, and some surprising yield on the other side of the initial investment. The same principle applies with people and causes. How do we continue to flourish when times are hard—emotionally, physically, spiritually? We receive dividends from the people we've sacrificially invested in.

Generally I believe that we should invest in people first and causes second. This is not a fast rigid rule but I try to abide by it when possible. Causes have a way of staying around or coming back around. But when you find a passionate leader who has attached their passion and calling to a cause, jump in with a sacrificial investment.

Giving to others infuses our own lives with blessing. I could be having a lousy day, and then receive an email from a friend I've invested my time and energy with over the years and find total blessing and lift simply from hearing about *his* progress and how God is blessing *him*. That's the beauty of pouring into others. That's how I flourish even when the days seem to be withering me away.

UNINHIBITED TRUST

Manley Beasley was one of a dozen mentors who profoundly impacted my life. He had the unmistakable gift of faith. He contracted several life-threatening diseases, but he trusted God each day to live. He hung his daily existence to a promise God had given him that he would live to see his grandchildren. In the face of pain, fear, and discouragement, Manley lived with these aliments in a bizarre and extreme show of faith. He learned how to throw his faith on Jesus, not his own ingenuity.

I will never forget the day, standing in an elevator in Memphis, when he asked me, "Steve, what are you trusting God for that if He doesn't come through you're totally sunk?" I stumbled and mumbled, looked one way, then the other, and finally muttered, "Nothing, I guess." I am convinced that we don't give sacrificially because we lack the trust to do so. We say we trust God, but when it comes to investing in others, we give to the point where we feel like we're still in control—no further. In doing so, however, we rob ourselves of the blessings God has for us. If we do indeed trust Him with everything, our giving and investing in people should show it. When I sacrificially give, I'm trusting in God to make up the difference. We don't give, because we don't trust.

Repeat this verse to yourself. "Trust in the Lord with all your heart ..." Now go and do it! I'll join you as we find friends and colleagues to invest in, to go deep with on their journey.

When others flourish, you flourish. And when you flourish, others will flourish. That's the truth. When you sacrificially invest in people of substance and matters of consequence, when you invest ahead of tangible returns or repayment, you are replanting yourself. Not only that, you're contributing to a flourishing culture. That's the power of investing in others. A spiritual or social ROI has just as much cultural impact as a financial one.

Oh, I did great things: built houses, planted vineyards, designed gardens and parks and planted a variety of fruit trees in them, made pools of water to irrigate the groves of trees.

I bought slaves, male and female, who had children, giving me even more slaves; then I acquired large herds and flocks, larger than any before me in Jerusalem. I piled up silver and gold, loot from kings and kingdoms. I gathered a chorus of singers to entertain me with song, and—most exquisite of all pleasures —voluptuous maidens for my bed.

Oh, how I prospered! I left all my predecessors in Jerusalem far behind, left them behind in the dust. What's more, I kept a clear head through it all. Everything I wanted I took—I never said no to myself. I gave in to every impulse, held back nothing. I sucked the marrow of pleasure out of every task—my reward to myself for a hard day's work! Then I took a good look at everything I'd done, looked at all the sweat and hard work. But when I looked, I saw nothing but smoke. Smoke and spitting into the wind. There was nothing to any of it. Nothing.

– Ecclesiastes 2:4-11 (MSG)

A LIFE DEVOTED TO THINGS
IS A DEAD LIFE, A STUMP;
A GOD-SHAPED LIFE IS A
FLOURISHING TREE.
– PROVERBS 11:28 (MSG)

CHAPTER 9

IN QUIET PLACES

*How Silence Makes
You Grow*

"Silence is the element in which great things fashion themselves together."– Thomas Carlyle

STOP. NO, REALLY, I want you to stop. Stop mentally reviewing tomorrow's to-do list. Stop replaying this morning's meeting in your head. Just stop. Don't stop reading, but stop spinning your wheels. Stop allowing the ideas and concerns and stresses of your life to destroy your chances of gleaning something worthwhile from this brief book.

It's not just you. I too have to make myself stop. To get outside the craziness of the everyday, I routinely create opportunities for space. I may consider a book or a talk I've listened to. I may ponder a conversation I've had with a friend or meditate on something I've learned from Scripture. Whatever it is, I consciously stop everything to do that one thing.

Over the years, no book has meant more to me in the area of developing spiritual disciplines than Chuck Swindoll's *So, You Want to Be Like Christ?* This book, which is an expanded edition of his earlier best seller *Intimacy with the Almighty*, is one of those books I pull off the shelf several times a year. It's the kind of book I buy in bulk and give to friends because of how much it's helped me grow spiritually.

Swindoll possesses a unique gift of being able to distill heavy theological truths into understandable and relevant prose. In his chapter on silence he challenges readers to pause. I'd like to draw from Swindoll on this topic because I find it so important in the process of learning and growing to be more like Christ. He focuses on the Old Testament word *selah*, a word used throughout the Psalms. The best translation for this word is "a pause." Swindoll's friend translates *selah* like this: "Pause, and let that sink in."

And that's what I'm asking you to do right now.

REFLECTION AND CONSIDERATION

Reflection and consideration precede meaningful authentic application. In our world of speed and instant-everything we too often consume books and meaningful information with whim and nonchalance. We pick up a book, hit the highlights, and move on. But if we can learn to exercise a bit of patience as we read and study, we will find—at least this is my experience—golden nuggets of truth waiting for us.

When you take the time to reflect and consider a portion of Scripture, or even a good book, there's usually a different kind of application available. It's easy to look at lists and bullet points and say, "Okay, great. I've got it." But when we do this, we only scratch the surface of the growth awaiting us. We merely consume the information, and any application will likely have something to do with me and go no further. If, however, we can slow down just a little, then we have the chance to become men and women of deliberate action through the conviction gained in the quiet recesses of reflection.

But vibrant growth concerns more than just you and me getting better. It's an ethos change, a way of life in which our perspectives shift from being a person consumed with "me, me, me" getting "better, better, better," to a person concerned with others discovering what we have discovered. Does that seem backwards to you?

It may, and that's okay; let me explain.

I've found silence to be not just a "thing" I experience but a way of life I try to cultivate. When I take time by the river, away from my anxious schedule, to-do list, and ringing phone,

I find myself exposed—face to face with my honest thoughts, fears, and dreams. When I jump on my bike on Saturday morning and ride 15 miles on the trails around the lake, it's a moment of selah—pause for me. It's in this vulnerable place I often meet with God, and it isn't a one-dimensional *kumbaya* kind of meeting. It's a business meeting with God that covers all aspects of life. For me, this quiet business meeting looks like this:

I must find my own cave. And no, no, I'm not a bear—although some of my closest friends might disagree! Finding your own cave is, quite simply, establishing *your place of retreat.* This is an essential first step toward the regularity of times of silence and growth. In order to meet with God, and reflect on life, family, and business you first need a place to go.

It should be a place you know, without a shadow of doubt, will afford you the space to do all the things we're discussing—things like reflecting, thinking, listening, resting, unloading, complaining, etc.

It must be a place that encourages you to unplug from the normal routine and engage in the experience of quiet, of retreat. Why is this so important? Because the point of retreating to your cave is to go somewhere familiar, somewhere that doesn't demand you buy a plane ticket, somewhere more immediate—a place you can easily etch into your calendar. It just so happens I have a couple of caves, places where I can retreat to on a regular basis. These familiar hideaways allow me to refresh my mind and heart, to refocus and reinvigorate what really matters most: my soul.

I capture my honest epiphanies and visit them often. You'd be hard pressed to find me without a Moleskine or a pad of some kind. Over the years I've really worked to develop the discipline of writing things down, especially in the quiet times of life. Researchers have found journaling to be therapeutic and healing. I find that when I write something down, I am more likely to return and reflect on it later.

Writing my thoughts down helps me see my thought pattern over a stretch of time. I can see how goals were reached over time, prayer requests answered, and I can gather a good sense for where God is leading me in terms of my career, giftedness, and family life.

Writing my thoughts down also provides me with a built-in accountability device. For example, when I write my goals down and return to them, I will either be encouraged by my progress or convicted of my laxity in an area. Accountability, though, consists of more than simply keeping track of the areas in which I need more and better work. It can also serve us by way of encouragement. Since my days in college I have practiced a discipline every Thanksgiving and Christmas season. Sometime during the holidays I reflect on the year about to close and the year about to open. And I write it down.

I have several friends who write professionally for a living. One of them recently told me that a good editor will not simply bleed red comments all over the page, telling you what you did wrong. Rather, a good editor will work with your voice, and find ways to undergird your voice with better structure and content direction and idea flow. I see this as a good kind of accountability. When I write things down and return to it, it acts as a kind of positive reinforcement for my financial goals, my career dreams, and my family vitality.

It's not just about writing goals down and working to cross them off. It's about processing. The quiet times of writing in my life have helped me process through some tough circumstances and have also helped me clarify my thoughts on issues I hold dear. It reaffirms what I've committed to and allows me to reevaluate how I plan to get there.

Next, my times of quiet do not center on a particular agenda. What I mean by that is in times of rest and quiet, I am not attempting to achieve anything in particular. I often recommend to the executives I coach to go spend some time being "non-productive." We are addicted to outcome in our culture. I believe the quiet life looks like a rhythmic life. If you constantly cultivate your life around the principles of silence, then certain by-products emerge.

Think of the small flower planted in spring. As a seedling it experiences a good bit of time in the cold dark earth. It's a quiet and life-giving time, and it's during that time the seedling births—a shoot works its way through the moist dirt and finds the sunlight. Once in the sunlight the growing flower encounters all the intensities of pure nature: rain, storm winds, flooding, the cold and the heat. It needs the sun. It needs the rain. It needs the air to continue its growth. But always, it must begin in the cool dark of silence.

In order for you and I to flourish, we must always return to the cool dark silence of quiet with God. Like the gritty earth, it is our genesis for growth. It is in this place of total quiet, a place of solitude, that we discover the value of no agendas, no outcomes. That sounds like a bit of heresy in a culture where outcomes, ROI, and "impact" saturate the business and leadership world.

We must, however, learn that thriving does not always entail achieving. We must spend time in the ground of growth. Even though each generation differs in their ability to enter into a time of quiet reflection, the benefit never disappears. The drive to achieve is very real, but it is the leaders who learn how to shelve those pressures in favor of times of quiet pause who thrive.

Finally, try and limit my digital communication use to basically nothing. Aside from a quick call to my wife to check in, I'm off the reservation. While this may sound like an obvious aspect of quiet retreat, the reality is quite different. In talking with young and seasoned professionals in every industry, almost everyone admits the difficulty of literally unplugging from their digital worlds for any amount of time.

Digital communication has become such a part of our work and play culture that we can hardly remember a time without smartphones and tablet computers. Test what I'm saying. This evening, don't open your tablet, don't turn on the television, don't answer your phone or texts, and don't get out your laptop. Instead, pour a glass of your favorite beverage and do something analog. Remember what analog means? What I mean by analog is something that does not require a plug or screen. Talk to an old friend or your spouse, read a book, write a letter or note of encouragement. Then, be honest with how hard it is in this day and age to unwind without unplugging.

My friend, Tim, recently moved to England. He told me how it took over three weeks for the local cable service to set up his rental house with Internet. On top of that, he didn't have a phone, and when he and his wife finally did get phones the reception was awful. Tim also chose not to buy a car and to rely on the mass transit alternative. For the first few weeks, he says, he felt anxious, like he should be doing something. Then he realized, he was so trained to go, go, go and browse, click, download, that when he actually *had* to unplug it felt unnatural.

"We felt anxious," Tim told me. "But we didn't know why. And then, after about three weeks of no car and very limited cell phone, we felt ourselves slow down. Our shoulders relaxed and we realized—*we don't have to do any of this, really.*"

For Tim and his family, they entered into a whole new era. He says it's like they're living in a kind of silence. It's a kind of quiet he associates with the unhinged and unplugged time of his younger years. He feels free, and he's unfettered with worry. The pace of life has slowed and he finds himself embracing it more and more—more walks in the countryside, more time talking with his wife, more writing.

In my opinion, that's what silence does to you and for you. It slows you down. It reminds you of a more innocent time of life. It brings out the youthfulness that so easily gets beaten down by the busyness of adulthood. When I'm in one of my "cave spots" I get lost on the river fishing.

Unplugging tends to slow down the way you think about things. In order to flourish in life, it's important to understand the value and power of strong thinking. Our culture tends to be a read and react kind of society. We watch, we interact, we disagree, we react, sometimes harshly and many times without thinking.

A flourishing mind waits. It sees the value in processing ideas and looks down the road at the big picture.

MORE THAN JUST A "QUIET TIME"

While I've spent some time describing what a retreat looks like—where you unplug from your normal schedule and refocus—I must tell you that flourishing demands more than just quick breaks of trout-fishing on the river. If you desire to flourish, you must adopt a flourishing lifestyle, of which rest is simply a part. I think it's possible to operate and achieve at a high level in this world—whether it's your job, your schooling, or your home life—and yet keep from running into the ground.

The idea of "seasons" comes up often when I talk to leaders

and friends. "I'm just in a really busy season, that's all. It will end soon, and then I'll get some R-and-R." I've said this before, and I'm sure you have as well. But it's possible to let the cycle of busy "seasons" define how we live. Here's what I mean.

A friend of mine once told me about his boss, who also happens to be a very successful businessman. This boss ran the "season life." He sprinted from one season to the next. He'd bury himself in work, keep insane hours, make heaps of money, and crash. It wasn't long, however, until the next season arrived, and off he went.

I call this kind of living the *Sprint Life*. It is not healthy. It isn't sustainable. It does not promote flourishing.

First of all, life is not a sprint. It's a marathon...maybe even an ultra-marathon. It demands pace, constant nourishment, and refreshment. It demands training and focus. Like any marathon, life will invariably have a few hills to climb and stretches of challenging training. And if you're hydrated and well trained, you'll struggle a bit, but you'll make it through. On the other hand, if you're not ready, and you've been burning all your energy in a sprint, you could cramp up, you could black out, you could fall.

My friend's boss developed diabetes, and struggles to keep his weight in a healthy place. He'll take off for a week, and then he's right back at it. I believe we're all different—each of us wired differently. But everyone, at some point, needs rest. Everyone needs to remain healthy.

The Sprint Life is a way of life that focuses on the wrong things. Even though it's after good things, like effectiveness, ROI, and achievement, the Sprint Life approaches them from the wrong perspective. The flourishing person goes about it differently, attacking life from the inside out.

So, though quiet times are essential to your overall

flourishing, the great need is what I call the *Silent Life*. I don't mean that we should walk around as monks. One of my favorite writers, the Apostle Paul, wrote a letter to the church in first century Thessalonica, where he addressed this matter. In it he reminded the people to *"make it your ambition to lead a quiet life: You should mind your own business and work with your hands"* (1 Thessalonians 4:11 NIV). Paul encourages people to work and to work hard, but to always remain mindful of the way you approach and go about that work.

I think we can learn something about flourishing from Paul. The Silent Life looks like you and me going hard after our individual calling in life, be it leadership in a company, a school teacher, a pastor, or a student. Whatever work we find worthy of our time, we should do it, and work hard at it. But working hard does not mean we work stupid. We don't sprint from season to season.

Instead, we take the principles of our silent retreats—those times when we go extreme and unplug from everything all at once—and work them into the everyday rhythms of our life. Put another way, we build rest and reflection into how we live life. We don't just take breaks when we're so burned out that we collapse. Instead, we proactively build a life infused with rest and avoid those extremes altogether. Maybe this means you "rest" from work each evening by turning off your email notifications after 6:00 p.m. Try leaving your phone in the kitchen when you go to bed. Or, perhaps you commit to being present with your family during dinner—no phones, computers, or TVs. Perhaps you get up 30 minutes early every morning to sit in the quiet of a sleeping house and reflect upon Scripture or pray. There is no right or wrong way to do it; the point is that you have to do it. I've often heard pastors preach spiritual discipline by reminding that no one "stumbles into holiness." Guess what, you aren't going to magically fall into a healthy rhythm of life. You've got to make it happen and keep it as a priority. If you do this over time, I promise you'll notice a change for the better.

Remember what my friend Tim said: After a few weeks of doing things differently, the anxiety ceased and he entered into a new era for himself and his family, a quiet time, a refreshing time, a time that he wants to keep. I believe we'd all benefit from a time of quiet evaluation. What rules our days, our weeks, our years? How fast are we really living? Maybe we don't even realize how fast we're going. And that's exactly why we should seek silence for a while. In that silence, in our caves, I believe we'll find our true selves. We'll remember how precious a walk can be, what the wind sounds like coming over the hills, what the sunrise feels like when viewed from the quiet corners of our cave. And as those things happen, we find ourselves in the path of flourishing.

THE RIGHTEOUS THRIVE
LIKE A PALM TREE AND
GROW LIKE A CEDAR TREE IN
LEBANON. PLANTED IN THE
HOUSE OF THE LORD, THEY
THRIVE IN THE COURTS OF
OUR GOD. THEY WILL STILL
BEAR FRUIT IN OLD AGE,
HEALTHY AND GREEN.
– PSALM 92:12-14 (HCSB)

CHAPTER 10

NO SILVER
BULLET

*A Lifelong Walk in
the Same Direction*

"Our motto must continue to be perseverance. And ultimately I trust the Almighty will crown our efforts with success." —William Wilberforce

WE'RE ALWAYS LOOKING for shortcuts. Faster routes to work with less traffic. Five easy steps to lose 10 pounds. Quick and simple meals that taste great. Even our phones and keyboards come preloaded with more shortcuts than we could ever use. Less work in less time with the same results. That's what we want.

But shortcuts don't work well in life, and they especially don't work well for the things that really matter. You can't hit the shortcut button to climb the corporate ladder or earn your graduate degree. There's no corner to cut to fix your marriage or heal from the loss of a loved one. You can't pull a fast life-judo move and find yourself in a state of flourishing. As a matter of fact, shortcuts are fundamentally antithetical to the flourishing life. The flourishing life takes time, and it takes work over time.

The flourishing life also requires intentionality. In the previous chapter I warned that no one magically falls into a healthy rhythm of rest in his or her life. The same applies to the flourishing life as a whole. You simply aren't going to happen upon it by accident. We don't run willy-nilly into the flourishing life. On the contrary, the flourishing life is a life of conscious choices and commitments, made and reaffirmed over time.

Be careful not to miss the "over time" part of that last statement, because it's critical. The most dangerous misconception about flourishing is that it's a destination. It's not. Flourishing is a state that we live in now *and* one that we are constantly working toward. If I want to flourish, and to do so over the long haul, then I must learn to hold these two concepts in tension: the flourishing of the moment and the goal I intend to reach or achieve.

I will never stay in a place of flourishing. I must always grow. I must always find myself in a season of pruning. I must always take time to deepen my roots in the barren times of winter that life throws at me.

A flourishing life is made up of an entirety of flourishing moments. All the moments of my life build and compound and grow into a life resembling a majestic maple tree—vast and spreading, deep and growing.

As you've probably already noticed, I love to fish. There are few things I enjoy more than getting lost fishing up and down a great small mouth bass or trout river. I remember watching great local anglers when I was a boy and immediately knowing that I wanted to catch big beautiful fish just like they did. So, one day, I showed up at a popular creek with all my fishing gear and started catching trophy fish all morning. Almost at once I achieved what I had dreamed about. I was a master fisherman.

Like most fishing stories, this one isn't even close to being true. I didn't just show up on a riverbank and start catching trout. I intentionally set out on a journey to *become* a fisherman. What's interesting, though, is that I would call myself a fisherman *and* I would say I am always becoming a fisherman. I'm always learning new tricks of the craft, new places to fish, and understanding how to best use my gear.

I didn't just show up with fishing gadgets and *Voila!* I set out with a specific goal and I continue to achieve that goal— the ever-growing, ever-learning fisherman.

If I desire a life of flourishing I'm not just going to show up

"I MUST ALWAYS TAKE TIME
TO DEEPEN MY ROOTS IN THE
BARREN TIMES OF WINTER
THAT LIFE THROWS AT ME."

and hope everything goes my way. I will put my hand to plow, as it were, and begin the daily intentional acts that accompany living life to the fullest.

THERE ARE NO "SCRATCH AND WIN" PLANS FOR LIFE

We live in a culture full of people looking for instant success—the one right move to take us over the top. It's why you know someone who has fallen for a pyramid scheme and why you've bought a Powerball ticket. I don't think it's because we're stupid, or lazy, or even greedy. I think it's because we are inherently drawn to the idea of a singular action that will set everything right. My experience, however, has shown that this sort of instant success is the exception, rather than the norm. Most successful people I've had the pleasure of working with didn't do one thing right, they did several things right *and* probably a few things wrong. They performed a series of moves over time that either allowed them to succeed or pushed them to failure, but always led them to understanding and maturity.

There is no silver bullet, scratch-and-win move that can catapult you into success in the material sense or in the flourishing sense of the word. You must not only be intentional about life, but you must also make hard decisions that move you toward the ever-present, always-ahead-of-your-goal of the flourishing life.

Winston Churchill, who was famous himself for never giving up, once said, "If you are going through hell, keep going." Sometimes when things get "thick" in life, you just have to keep going. When you keep suffering setbacks at work or you run into wall after wall trying to connect with your teenage kid, sometimes you just have to put your head down and put one foot in front of the other. This is often what life demands. We cannot simply step out of life because things don't go as planned.

The Apostle Paul knew this better than most. Shipwrecked, blinded, persecuted, and chased, he reminded us that we must endure. It's part of a special ethical hierarchy of living, or what I like to call my Guide to Hope. Paul, in what may seem an odd turn, began by suggesting that we rejoice when life throws pain and suffering our way. We should rejoice because we inherently understand that suffering produces endurance. Endurance, then, produces character—it makes you a better person. Finally, character produces hope.

It is the person of character, the person who has endured, the person who has suffered who is the person of hope. Paul wasn't just saying, "Buck up!" Rather, he was doing something uncommon in his culture. He was saying, "When the going gets tough, it is the wise person who remains tranquil, who remains steady."

From the wisest among us to the most foolish, deep down we understand that there is no quick trip to success. We understand that to live is to struggle. We must remember, though, that struggle begets success. In life, the truly successful people are the ones who have paid their dues and did their fair share of fighting along the way. You won't win in life with one quick takedown. But you can win in life by fighting through each struggle, holding on to hope one moment at a time, and continually moving toward the flourishing horizon.

CONTEXT, CONTEXT, CONTEXT

"That sounds great, Steve, but you don't know my situation…my company…my family…my difficult employees…my competition…my unruly children…my financial situation…my life."

Whether I'm coaching a client, grabbing coffee with an old friend, or offering guidance to a young entrepreneur, I often hear some version of this statement. In fact, this very thought seems to be the default response from most of us when anyone tries to inject a little wisdom into our world. What's interesting is that these responses, which may at first appear dismissive, do not usually emerge because we don't want the wisdom or because we don't think it's actually very wise. The issue, more often than not, is contextualization.

We *want* to apply the great application point from last week's sermon to our lives. We *want* to align our life with the truths of Scripture. We *want* to use the advice given by our boss during our review. We *want* to take what we see working in the lives of those we admire and apply it to our own life… but, we can't. Why?

Because contextualization is hard. It's not easy to take scriptural truth, parenting wisdom, or strategic guidance and apply it to our own unique context, and your context is unique. I often say that strategy and useful strategy are not the same thing. Useful strategy includes context, trust, and deep subject matter expertise. Context is huge. Even if the details of your work or family or ministry situation may be similar to that of another person, you are unique. Your voice, your createdness, is unique. What it means for you to flourish is unique, and you must figure it out.

So, as you read through the last pages of this short book and consider how you might more fully embrace the abundant life that Christ came to provide, be conscious of your context and remember two things. First, as you take whatever wisdom you (hopefully) have gleaned and attempt to apply it to your life, remember that nourishing rest or silence or community probably looks different for you than it does for me. If you find silence in the quiet of the morning with a cup of coffee and the sunrise, that's great; set your alarm and get up early. If, however, your silence is found in a long run just after the sun goes down and the crickets start chirping, that's fine too...lace up your shoes and go. The personalized discipline is what is important, not how it is manifested.

Second, remember to never allow your context to become an excuse for not flourishing. To put it another way, regardless of how rest or silence or community may look in your life, YOU need rest and silence and community to flourish. No matter how difficult your situation may be, no matter how lousy your job is or disobedient your kids are, God desires for you to flourish. Your situation can never disqualify you from the abundant life.

The Apostle Paul embodied this truth more fully than perhaps anyone. Here's a quick recap of his unique context:

> ...beaten times without number, often in danger of death. Five times I received from the Jews thirty-nine lashes. Three times I was beaten with rods, once I was stoned, three times I was shipwrecked, a night and a day I have spent in the deep. I have been on frequent journeys, in dangers from rivers, dangers from robbers, dangers from my countrymen, dangers from the Gentiles, dangers in the city, dangers in the wilderness, dangers on the sea, dangers among false brethren; I have been in labor and hardship, through many sleepless nights, in hunger and thirst, often without food, in cold and exposure. Apart from such external things, there is the daily pressure on me of concern for all the churches (2 Corinthians 11:23-28 NASB).

And yet...Paul flourished. Through all these unique pressures and challenges he thrived and fulfilled the calling set before him in a profound way. Why can't we?

"FOR I KNOW THE PLANS I HAVE FOR YOU,"—THIS IS THE LORD'S DECLARATION—"PLANS FOR YOUR WELFARE, NOT FOR DISASTER, TO GIVE YOU A FUTURE AND A HOPE."

– JEREMIAH 29:11 (HCSB)

CONCLUSION

I LOVE TREES. I have ten maples, four Bradford pears, three dogwoods, and, most recently, a magnolia (man, this ought to be a country song). My wife and I planted these trees over the years, during which we had to navigate ice and wind storms, a new construction development behind our property, droughts, heat waves, cul-de-sac kids' adventures, and super-ninja moles.

The maples rise tall and proud. Like proud soldiers hoisting their flags after victory, they wave their leaves in a cascading symphony of fiery colors. First the bright yellows peak, and then the oranges burst forth, followed finally by the rich reds. It's magnificent to watch these beauties flourish—from the first buds of spring to the dying hues of fall to the barren limbs of winter.

Big Red (as I call him) is the grandest of our maples. He sits on the north side of my house, where he keeps watch and blankets my yard with his deep crimson foliage in the autumn months. I find his strength and stature arresting. Every year I water him and wait for the declaration.

Contrast Big Red with the young and fragile magnolia outside the kitchen window. It's only a couple of years old, and it's struggling to establish its roots and trying to endure the wind from our intense southern storms. I want the little guy to take root and drink deep the minerals and nutrients it needs to flourish. The magnolia is not the opposite of Big Red; it's simply young. The jury's still out on whether it will flourish and thrive.

Anyone can plant a tree. But in the words of Ezekiel, "but will it flourish?" Planting a tree doesn't mean the tree will reach its potential. A flourishing tree is full and vibrant, thriving and fruitful, whereas a withering tree produces no fruit, and looks sparse and spindly. In order to flourish, the tree needs to tap a

"A FLOURISHING TREE
IS FULL AND VIBRANT,
THRIVING AND FRUITFUL,
WHEREAS A WITHERING TREE
PRODUCES NO FRUIT, AND
LOOKS SPARSE AND SPINDLY."

plentiful source of water, establish deep roots, and have space to grow in the sunlight.

Trees astound me. They rise up in all directions, reaching for pockets of sunshine. They dig deep and burrow for water. And all the while they give and give and give. They give fruit. They give shade. They give wonder. They give beauty. They even give in death as material for building and fuel for warmth.

A thriving tree gives us a symbol of what a flourishing life might look like: well established, strong, constantly growing, enduring through the seasons of life, and giving to others.

We all need watering, nourishment, and support. Especially leaders. Leading is lonely, confusing, scary, exhausting, risky, and often full of difficult circumstances. In the face of these challenges, what will tether us to the abundance, support, and nourishment that we so vitally need?

As humans, and especially as followers of Christ, we must be intentional about our personal growth. We cannot simply plug in to the world's patterns and definitions of success and expect to emerge at the end of our lives fulfilled and joyful. Jesus' most famous sermon, often called "The Sermon on the Mount," is largely a list of things that most people think about wrongly, followed by Jesus' explanation of the right way to see those things. Without doubt, Jesus was trying to adjust our baseline to amend our pursuit of true flourishing.

I'm fortunate to have sat under outstanding mentors who watered me and pruned me. I've had the joy of growing alongside friends who've cared for me and nurtured me through their wisdom and sacrificial love. Through it all, I've experienced plenty of failures and disappointments—more than I care to share, really. Both come with flourishing; both are needed to make us strong. Through it all, I held on to hope. Hope, for me, was a vision of what *could be* in my life and work. I believe leaders need to be men and women of hope—able to see what others cannot.

I hope you have hope too. I hope you have not given up on your desire to flourish. As long as there is life, there is the possibility to start over again. And the offer for an abundant life never expires.

BUT I AM LIKE A
FLOURISHING OLIVE TREE
IN THE HOUSE OF GOD;
I TRUST IN GOD'S FAITHFUL
LOVE FOREVER AND EVER.
–PSALM 52:8 (HCSB)

*REFLECTION
QUESTIONS*

CHAPTER 1

1. Would you describe your life as something that you are "surviving through" or "thriving in"? Why?
2. In what areas of your life are you "getting by" rather than "flourishing"?
3. Circle the words that best describe your life as a whole:
   a. Exhausted OR Energized
   b. Empty OR Overflowing
   c. Lost OR Purposeful
   d. Withered OR Thriving
   e. Hindered OR Breaking Forth
4. What friends and leaders have captivated you with the impact and vibrancy of their life? What, in particular, makes their lives so compelling to you?
5. Which aspect of Aristotle's "flourishing" definition are you lacking most acutely? (Enduring happiness, penetrating wisdom, optimal well-being, authentic love and compassion)
6. Is the happiness in your life enduring or fleeting?
7. Do you think your understanding of the flourishing life matches with what Jesus spoke of in John 10:10?

CHAPTER 2

1. How much do your hopes of flourishing depend upon material success?

2. Toward which version of the "Prosperity Gospel" are you working?

3. How would you answer Paul's question, "Am I now seeking the approval of man, or of God?"

4. How well do your ambitions line up with the ambitions of God?

5. How content are you? What is preventing you from embracing contentment regardless of circumstances?

6. Are you trusting God in all areas of your life? Or are there some areas you have held too tightly?

7. How holistic is your view of prosperity? What might you be neglecting?

CHAPTER 3

---

1. Do you buy that we all have a created unique voice deposited in us by our Maker?

2. How well attuned are you to your unique voice?

3. What are you good at that many people struggle with? What do you struggle with that many people seemingly do with ease?

4. How well does your "voice" and your "career" line up?

5. In your life right now, do you feel more like David wearing his shepherd's clothes, holding his sling OR more like David in Saul's heavy armor?

6. What are you making prominent with your voice? Yourself? Others? God?

7. If your current job doesn't line up with your voice, what are you doing about it?

CHAPTER 4

1. What happens to us when we try to "know it all, be it all, and do it all"?
2. What are your callings?
3. Which callings are you excelling in? Which are you neglecting?
4. Have you mastered the "art of the swap"? Is there anything on your table right now that needs to be swapped for something else?
5. How do you balance the idea of "multiple callings" and the unrealistic pursuit of perfection?
6. Do you know what your life rhythm should look and sound like? What tweaks can you make to get in better rhythm?
7. Do you struggle with sorting between a good idea, a divine mandate, and culture expectation?

CHAPTER 5

1. Are you at peace with the inherent risks of your life and work? If not, what risks cause you the most anxiety?
2. What makes up your root system? How deep do they run?
3. What are you doing to nourish and strengthen your roots?

4. Are you experiencing life-giving community? With whom?
5. What is the most challenging part of building and maintaining community for you?
6. How did your roots hold up the last time your life "hit a wall"?
7. Which root system is stronger? Your interior roots or your exterior roots?

CHAPTER 6

1. Do you have a "long view" of life?
2. How have you allowed the speed and immediacy of our culture to shorten your perspective?
3. How do you process failure? Success?
4. Have you ever flourished through difficult circumstances? How did you do it?
5. What are you investing in right now that will outlive you?
6. Which aspect of a long view do you struggle with? Living with the past? Wading through the present? Looking around the bend to the future?
7. What do you have hope in? How constant is that hope?

1. How active is your love? Does it rest with you, or does it grow in you and move outward?
2. Which individuals in your life know you well AND love you well?
3. Which individuals do YOU know well and love well?
4. Whose narrative do you value as much as your own?
5. How well do you understand your motives? Why do we do the things we do?
6. Does your understanding of "neighbor" match God's? Who do you love that doesn't love you or is not really lovable?
7. How has love compelled you to act? For what purposes were you compelled?

CHAPTER 8

1. Who do you have energy for that isn't you?
2. Are you a relational giver OR taker? Where can you sharpen your giving skills?
3. In your life, who has had energy for you?
4. How well are you reflecting the goodness God has imprinted upon you?
5. In what ways is your giving hampering or pinching you? Are there things that you would like to do, but cannot do because of your giving?

6. How has helping others flourish affected your flourishing?
7. How complete is your trust in God? What areas are you holding back?

CHAPTER 9

1. When was the last time you felt truly rested?
2. What are you regularly spending time reflecting on and considering? Scripture? Sermons? Books? Poetry?
3. How do you find times of silence in your life?
4. Where is your cave? Do you have a place you can retreat to and rest?
5. Are you capturing the fruits of your rest and reflection? How?
6. Do you have any times in your day or week that you limit your digital communication?
7. Is rest a part of your regular life rhythm? If not, how can you weave healthy rest and silence into your life?

CHAPTER 10

1. Do you have a plan for your flourishing life? Is it a long-term or a short-term plan?
2. What have you learned or been reminded of from this book that you can apply immediately to your own life?

3. Are you inherently drawn to "quick fixes" in life? Why do you think that is true?

4. What hard decisions do you need to make to move toward a flourishing life?

5. What aspects of your unique situation have you allowed to act as barriers to a flourishing life? How can you remove or overcome those?

6. What is one practical way you can apply a principle from this book to your context?

7. Write a "Prayer of Flourishing" to guide your daily life. Engage it daily.

NOTES

1. John Eldredge, *Wild At Heart* (Nashville: Thomas Nelson, 2001), 18.
2. This is the common definition for human flourishing as taken from Aristotle's fourth century lectures, which later came to be known as Nicomachean Ethics.
3. *Harvard Business Review*, July/August 2010.
4. David Lang, ed., *Assorted Quotations* (Accordance electronic ed. Altamonte Springs: OakTree Software, 2001), n.p.
5. C.S. Lewis, *The Weight of Glory* (HarperOne, 2009).
6. Richard Foster, *Prayer* (Zondervan, 2002).
7. C. S. Lewis, *Mere Christianity*, 1952.
8. C. S. Lewis, *The Screwtape Letters*. HarperOne: 2009
9. *http://www.inc.com/magazine/20011201/23735.html*
10. Rod Dreher, *The Little Way of Ruthie Leming* (Grand Central Publishers: New York, 2013), 266-267.
11. Ibid.
12. Carl Sandburg, *Abraham Lincoln: The Prairie Years and The War Years* (Harcourt: 1939).
13. C. S. Lewis, *Surprised by Joy: The Shape of My Early Life* (New York; London: Harcourt Brace, 1995), 210.
14. Jeffrey Marx, *Season of Life* (Simon & Schuster, 2004), p. 43.
15. Brennan Manning, *The Furious Longing of God* (David C. Cook, 2009).
16. C. S. Lewis, *Mere Christianity* (San Francisco; Harper, 2009).

My life and work in general and this book project in particular is richer because of a few friends. Having friends to help on a project only makes the work more enjoyable and the outcome more valuable. Solomon was right in Ecclesiastes 4. Two are better than one and three is amazing if you are ever able to enjoy that.

Tim Willard, Sean Dewitt, and Andrew Brill have put a ton of effort into helping produce this book. Actually it doesn't stop with three. Thank you Celeste, Donna, and Joel for all your work as well.

My writing world flourishes more because of you guys.

Steve is the founder of Coaching by Cornerstone, where he advises executives, business owners, and young entrepreneurs. When he isn't working his day job (or fishing), Steve writes and speaks often on topics related to strategy, work, and faith. After publishing the *Life@Work Magazine* some years ago, Steve recently launched a new writing and publishing venture, *stephenrgraves.com*. Through this venture, Steve is committed to drive conversations, extract insights, and publish around four themes of personal passion and curiosity: **Leadership Development, Social Innovation, Practical Faith,** and **Organizational Strategy**. To learn more, check out his weekly blog and look for the next book coming out soon.

For more resources from KJK Inc. Publishing, go to *stephenrgraves.com*

Other titles from Stephen R. Graves:

Notes